GLOBE EDUCATION
SHORTER SHAKESPEARE

A MIDSUMMER NIGHT'S DREAM

- Get straight to the heart of the play
- Understand the whole story
- Read Shakespeare's language with confidence

HODDER
EDUCATION
AN HACHETTE UK COMPANY

Introduction

Shakespeare the writer

Shakespeare would probably be amazed that you are studying one of his plays in school over 400 years after his death. He did not write his plays to be read, he wrote them to be performed. When he wrote, he expected a company of skilful actors to interpret and perform his play for an audience to listen to and watch. *A Midsummer Night's Dream* was printed in his lifetime, but eighteen of his plays were only printed after his death in a collection of his plays known as the *First Folio*.

Prose and verse

Most of the time, Shakespeare wrote *blank verse* – verse where the ends of the lines do not rhyme. So what makes it verse? It has a rhythm. Normally there are ten syllables in every line. Shakespeare wrote the lines to be spoken with the stress on every second syllable. Try saying,

"*baa-**boom** baa-**boom** baa-**boom** baa-**boom** baa-**boom***".

Moving on to a line from *A Midsummer Night's Dream*, try saying it with the same rhythm and stress:

"*So **will** – I **grow**, – so **live**, – so **die**, – my **lord**,*"

Shakespeare can break the rules of blank verse, but he does not often do so in *A Midsummer Night's Dream*. He does use prose instead of verse. Less socially important characters often speak in prose, as do comic characters. In *A Midsummer Night's Dream* the workmen who plan to put on a play are both, and they speak in prose – except when they are preforming their play.

Shared lines: Sometimes Shakespeare had two characters share the ten syllables that make a line (as Hippolyta and Theseus do on the right). He did this when he wanted the actors to keep the rhythm going. This was often to show the characters are particularly close, or when one is impatient.

Hippolyta	Four days will quickly steep themselves in night,	5
	Four nights will quickly dream away the time,	
	And then the moon, like to a silver bow	
	New-bent in heaven, shall behold the night	
	Of our solemnities.	
Theseus	Go Philostrate,	
	Stir up the Athenian youth to merriments,	10

Counting lines: You can see the number 5 at the end of the first line above right. It is normal to print the line number every five lines in a Shakespeare play. This helps people find an exact place when talking or writing about the play. If you count, however, you will see that line 10 is six lines after line 5 – the two lines that make the shared line only count as one.

Act and Scene: Printed plays are divided into Acts and Scenes. On the stage there is no real gap – a new scene happens when the story moves on, either to a new time or place. When Shakespeare's company performed indoors by candlelight they needed to trim the candles about every half an hour, so they picked points in the story where a short gap between scenes made sense. These became the divisions between Acts.

Elision: Elision is the correct term in English Literature for leaving a bit out. Shakespeare does it a lot. Often he can not quite fit what he wants to say into his ten-syllable line, so he cheats – running two words together. In the highlighted examples do not say *it is*, say *'tis* – the inverted comma shows you there is something missing.

Act 5 Scene 1

Enter Theseus, Hippolyta, with Philostrate and other lords and attendants.

Hippolyta   'Tis strange, my Theseus, that these lovers speak of.
More strange than true. I never may believe
These antic fables, nor these fairy toys.

Stage Directions: Shakespeare wrote stage directions – mainly when characters enter or exit, but sometimes telling actors what to do. In this book we develop Shakespeare's stage directions a bit, to tell you what you would see if you were watching the play.

Some stage directions are in square brackets, we print them as part of an actor's lines. These help you understand who the actor is talking to – which would be obvious on stage. *Aside* is a significant one – this is when the character shares their thoughts with the audience.

Enter Puck, unseen by the others on stage.

Puck   *[Aside.]* What hempen homespuns have we swagg'ring here,
So near the cradle of the Fairy Queen?
What, a play toward? I'll be an auditor,

45   **and so every one:** and you all do that

46   **hempen homespuns:** stupid peasants (only poor people wore the scratchy cloth made from hemp)

The glossary: Some words and phrases have changed their meaning or fallen out of use since Shakespeare's time. The glossary helps you with them. It gives you the line numbers in the play (in red); then the word, or the start and end of a long phrase (with three dots to mark the elision where some words have been left out), in **bold**; then the explanation in modern English. It is as close to the original line as we can make it.

Oberon drugs Titania, who is sleeping next to the Indian Boy, lines 14–20. How does what the audience sees of Titania contrast with what Oberon says?

1 As Oberon pours the juice into Titania's eyes, what do his words tell the audience about his character?

The questions: There are questions in the photo captions, and in red boxes. Here are two tips for answering them:

- There usually is not a simple 'right' answer. We hope you will develop your own ideas. The best way to answer any question is to back up your answer with a reference to the play text.

- Unless we tell you otherwise, you can answer the question using the play text on the opposite page.

Heavens

Upper stage

Stage

Galleries

Entrances

Yard

The Globe Theatre

Today's *Shakespeare's Globe* in London was built to show us what open-air theatres were like in Shakespeare's time. It is very different from other modern theatres. Shakespeare wrote *A Midsummer Night's Dream* for the original *Globe* theatre – so how was the play affected by the theatre it was written for?

- **The stage** was large, and stuck out into the audience, who surround it on three sides. The theatre was open-air, but a roof over the stage, called the *Heavens*, kept the actors (and their expensive costumes) dry if it rained. Two large pillars held up this roof, and the actors had to move around them.

- **The upper stage** was a balcony running along the back wall of the stage. Actors and musicians could use it. Also, it was the most expensive place for members of the audience to sit (people who sat there could seen by the rest of the audience in their fine clothes).

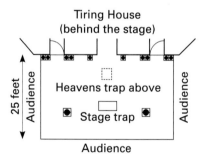

The stage trap opened into the area under the stage. The heavens trap was not on the stage, but above it. Actors playing gods might be lowered down to the stage through it.

Sam Wanamaker, an American actor and director, founded the Shakespeare's Globe Trust in 1970. Sam could not understand why there was not a proper memorial to the world's greatest playwright in the city where he had lived and worked. He started fundraising to build a new Globe Theatre. Sadly, Sam died before the theatre opened in 1997.

- **The entrances** were in the back wall of the stage, leading from the *Tiring House* (the actors' dressing room). There was a big door in the middle and a smaller door on either side. The big entrance was useful for bringing on large props like the flowery bed in Act 2 Scene 2.

- **Traps** allowed props or actors to appear or disappear from the Heavens or into the stage. The stage trap opened into the area under the stage. The Heavens trap was not on the stage, but above it, in the Heavens.

- **The audience** The theatre held well over 2,000 people (today's Globe holds 1,700). All the audience were close to the stage. People could pay a penny to stand in the open air in the Yard around the stage. Three tiers of roofed Galleries surrounded the Yard, where, for more money, people could sit on benches.

- **Sound, light and scenery** – there was not any, except for daylight, live music, and live sound effects (like rolling a cannonball in a trough to make a sound like thunder). The Globe was not dark, like a modern theatre; the actors and audience could all see each other – all the time. Shakespeare often started a play with a dramatic and noisy moment to grab the audience's attention. Characters often describe where they are, or that it was dark – see lines 305–309 of Act 3 Scene 2 (page 63).

The full text of part of Act 2 Scene 1 (lines 41–68), showing the cuts in the *Shorter Shakespeare* text.

Puck	Thou speak'st aright, I am that merry wand'rer of the night. I jest to Oberon and make him smile When I a fat and bean-fed horse beguile, Neighing in likeness of a filly foal. ~~And sometime lurk I in a gossip's bowl, In very likeness of a roasted crab, And when she drinks, against her lips I bob, And on her withered dewlap pour the ale.~~ The wisest aunt telling the saddest tale, Sometime for three-foot stool mistaketh me, Then slip I from her bum, down topples she, And "tailor" cries, and falls into a cough. ~~And then the whole choir hold their hips and laugh, And waxen in their mirth, and sneeze, and swear A merrier hour was never wasted there.~~ But room, Fairy! Here comes Oberon.	45 50 55
Fairy	And here my mistress. Would that he were gone!	
	Enter Oberon with his attendants at one door, and Titania with her attendants at another.	
Oberon	Ill met by moonlight, proud Titania.	60
Titania	What, jealous Oberon? Fairies skip hence: I have forsworn his bed and company.	
Oberon	Tarry, rash wanton. Am not I thy lord?	
Titania	Then I must be thy la~~dy. But I know When thou hast stol'n away from Fairy Land, And in the shape of Corin sat all day, Playing on pipes of corn and versing love To amorous Phillida.~~ Why art thou here,	65

What is 'Shorter Shakespeare'?

In the texts that survive, Shakespeare's plays are of very different lengths. The longest is 3,904 lines, and the shortest 1,918 lines (*A Midsummer Night's Dream* is 2,222 lines). Plays were said to take about two hours in Shakespeare's time (3,900 lines would take about 4 hours), so his company must have *cut* the play for performance. This could have meant leaving out whole scenes, and/or shortening speeches throughout the play. Almost all productions of Shakespeare's plays ever since have made some cuts to the text.

Shorter Shakespeare cuts the play to help you study it in the classroom. Our cut is about 1,200 lines, and we have 'filleted' the text, so you get all the important parts. We do not add to, or change, the words – Shakespeare originally wrote them all. The example on the left shows you the sort of things we have cut (from Act 2 Scene 1, page 23).

Theseus (left) and Hippolyta (in handcuffs)
What do the costumes of these two
characters suggest about them?
Why has the director chosen to have
Hippolyta in handcuffs?

Doubling

In Shakespeare's time, actors often played more than one part in the same play, because there were more parts than
actors in the company. This system was called 'doubling'. The audience was not expected to notice it. However, many
modern productions of *A Midsummer Night's Dream* double the parts of Theseus/Oberon and Hippolyta/Titania in a
deliberate doubling that the audience is meant to notice. This is because Theseus/Oberon and Hippolyta/Titania are the
rulers of their worlds, and in the play there are similarities between their position and the challenges they face.

Act 1 Scene 1

Enter Theseus, Hippolyta, Philostrate, and others.

Theseus	Now, fair Hippolyta, our nuptial hour
	Draws on apace. Four happy days bring in
	Another moon. But O, methinks, how slow
	This old moon wanes! She lingers my desires.
Hippolyta	Four days will quickly steep themselves in night, 5
	Four nights will quickly dream away the time,
	And then the moon, like to a silver bow
	New-bent in heaven, shall behold the night
	Of our solemnities.
Theseus	Go Philostrate,
	Stir up the Athenian youth to merriments, 10
	Turn melancholy forth to funerals. *Philostrate exits.*
	Hippolyta, I woo'd thee with my sword,
	And won thy love doing thee injuries.
	But I will wed thee in another key,
	With pomp, with triumph, and with revelling. 15

Enter Egeus, his daughter Hermia, Lysander,
and Demetrius.

Egeus	Happy be Theseus, our renowned Duke.
Theseus	Thanks good Egeus. What's the news with thee?
Egeus	Full of vexation come I, with complaint
	Against my child, my daughter Hermia. —
	Stand forth, Demetrius. — My noble lord, 20
	This man hath my consent to marry her. —
	Stand forth, Lysander. — And my gracious Duke,
	This man hath bewitch'd the bosom of my child.
	Thou, thou, Lysander, thou hast given her rhymes,
	And interchanged love-tokens with my child. 25
	Thou hast by moonlight at her window sung
	With feigning voice verses of feigning love.
	And stol'n the impression of her fantasy
	With bracelets of thy hair, rings, gauds, conceits,
	With cunning hast thou filched my daughter's heart, 30
	Turned her obedience (which is due to me)
	To stubborn harshness. And, my gracious Duke,
	Be it so she will not here, before your Grace,
	Consent to marry with Demetrius,
	I beg the ancient privilege of Athens. 35
	As she is mine, I may dispose of her,
	Which shall be either to this gentleman,
	Or to her death, according to our law
	Immediately provided in that case.

1–2 our nuptial hour Draws on apace: it will soon be our wedding day

2–3 Four happy days … Another moon: only four days until the new moon

4 wanes: wears itself out

5 steep themselves in: dissolve into

7 silver bow: refers to the shape of the new moon. It may also refer to to Diana, Roman goddess of hunting, the moon and chastity

9 solemnities: wedding ceremonies

12–3 I woo'd thee … doing thee injuries: I captured you in war

15 pomp … triumph … revelling: expensive public celebration

18 vexation: anger

23 bewitch'd …my child: charmed her heart away

27 feigning: twice in the line for a double meaning: 1) soft; 2) deceitful

28 stol'n the impression of her fantasy: made her think of nothing but him

29 gauds, conceits: cheap, flashy presents

30 filched: stolen

33 Be it so: if

35 ancient privilege: traditional legal right

39 Immediately … that case: written to deal with just this situation

Hermia
What do the expression on her face and her body language tell you about what she is feeling? What words of hers in the text support your answer?

1 How do the words used by Hermia, Egeus and Theseus show an audience how daughters were treated by their parents?

Theseus	What say you, Hermia? Be advised fair maid,
	To you your father should be as a god.
	One that composed your beauties, yea and one
	To whom you are but as a form in wax
	By him imprinted, and within his power
	To leave the figure or disfigure it.
	Demetrius is a worthy gentleman.
Hermia	So is Lysander.
Theseus	In himself he is.
	But in this kind, wanting your father's voice,
	The other must be held the worthier.
Hermia	I would my father looked but with my eyes.
Theseus	Rather your eyes must with his judgment look.
Hermia	I do entreat your grace to pardon me.
	I know not by what power I am made bold,
	But I beseech your Grace that I may know
	The worst that may befall me in this case,
	If I refuse to wed Demetrius.
Theseus	Either to die the death, or to abjure
	For ever the society of men.
	Therefore, fair Hermia, question your desires,
	Know of your youth, examine well your blood,
	Whether (if you yield not to your father's choice)
	You can endure the livery of a nun.
Hermia	So will I grow, so live, so die, my lord,
	Ere I will yield my virgin patent up
	Unto his lordship, whose unwishèd yoke
	My soul consents not to give sovereignty.
Theseus	Take time to pause, and, by the next new moon,
	(The sealing-day betwixt my love and me
	For everlasting bond of fellowship)
	Upon that day either prepare to die
	For disobedience to your father's will,
	Or else to wed Demetrius, as he would,
	Or on Diana's altar to protest
	For aye, austerity and single life.
Demetrius	Relent, sweet Hermia, and Lysander, yield
	Thy crazèd title to my certain right.
Lysander	You have her father's love, Demetrius,
	Let me have Hermia's. Do you marry him.
Egeus	Scornful Lysander! True, he hath my love,
	And what is mine, my love shall render him.
	And she is mine, and all my right of her
	I do estate unto Demetrius.

Line numbers: 40, 45, 50, 55, 60, 65, 70, 75, 80

40 **Be advised:** take my advice
42 **composed your beauties:** made you as you are
43–4 **but as a form … imprinted:** nothing but a wax figure he's made
48 **in this kind:** in these circumstances
48 **wanting:** without
48 **voice:** support
50 **I would:** I wish
51 **Rather:** instead
52 **I do entreat:** I beg
55 **befall me:** happen to me
57–8 **abjure For … of men:** become a nun
60 **Know of your youth:** think how young you are
60 **your blood:** your feelings, passions
61 **yield not to:** don't accept
62 **livery:** uniform
64 **ere I will … up:** before I give up my virginity
65–6 **whose unwishèd … sovereignty:** who I don't want to marry, and have to obey
67 **pause:** think it over
68 **sealing-day:** wedding day
68 **betwixt:** between
72 **as he would:** as your father wants
73–4 **on Diana's … single life:** to enter a nunnery forever
78 **Do you:** why don't you?
80 **render:** give to
82 **estate unto:** legally transfer to

Lysander and Hermia
What impression do the actors give of the relationship between Lysander and Hermia?

Lysander	I am, my lord, as well derived as he,
	As well possessed. My love is more than his.
	And, which is more than all these boasts can be, 85
	I am beloved of beauteous Hermia.
	Why should not I then prosecute my right?
	Demetrius, I'll avouch it to his head,
	Made love to Nedar's daughter, Helena,
	And won her soul. And she, sweet lady, dotes, 90
	Devoutly dotes, dotes in idolatry,
	Upon this spotted and inconstant man.
Theseus	I must confess that I have heard so much,
	And with Demetrius thought to have spoke thereof.
	For you, fair Hermia, look you arm yourself 95
	To fit your fancies to your father's will,
	Or else the law of Athens yields you up
	To death, or to a vow of single life. —
	Come my Hippolyta, what cheer, my love? —
	Demetrius and Egeus go along, 100
	I must employ you in some business
	Against our nuptial.
Egeus	With duty and desire we follow you.

They all exit, except Lysander and Hermia.

Lysander	How now, my love? Why is your cheek so pale?
	How chance the roses there do fade so fast? 105
Hermia	Belike for want of rain, which I could well
	Beteem them from the tempest of my eyes.
Lysander	Ay me! For aught that I could ever read,
	Could ever hear by tale or history,
	The course of true love never did run smooth, 110
	But either it was different in blood —
Hermia	O cross! Too high to be enthralled to low.
Lysander	Or else it stood upon the choice of friends —
Hermia	O hell! To choose love by another's eyes.
Lysander	Or, if there were a sympathy in choice, 115
	War, death, or sickness did lay siege to it.
Hermia	Then let us teach our trial patience,
	Because it is a customary cross,
	As due to love as thoughts and dreams and sighs,
	Wishes and tears, poor Fancy's followers. 120
Lysander	A good persuasion. Therefore hear me, Hermia,
	I have a widow aunt, a dowager
	Of great revenue, and she hath no child.
	From Athens is her house remote se'en leagues,
	There, gentle Hermia, may I marry thee, 125

83 as well derived: from as good a family
84 As well possessed: as rich
87 prosecute my right: press you let me marry Hermia
88 avouch it to his head: say it to his face
89 Made love to: courted
90 dotes: loves madly
91 dotes in idolatry: worships as a god
92 spotted: immoral
94 thereof: about it
95 look you arm yourself: prepare yourself
96 fit your fancies: shape your wishes
99 what cheer: what's the matter?
102 Against our nuptial: to do with the wedding
106 Belike: probably
107 Beteem: flood
107 tempest of my eyes: tears
108 For aught: from anything
111 it was different in blood: the lovers were from different social classes
112 O cross!: what a burden!
112 too high ... to low: too important to be married to someone of lower birth
113 stood upon: depended on
113 friends: relatives
115 if there ... choice: if the lovers could choose each other
117 teach ... patience: put up with it
118 a customary cross: the normal fate of lovers
119 As due to: as much a part of
120 Fancy's: love's (seen as a person)
122–3 a dowager Of great revenue: a rich widow
124 remote se'en leagues: seven leagues (21 miles) away

Helena

Study the actor's body language and expression. Which of these lines is she likely to be speaking: lines 141–2, lines 150–1, or line 157? Explain the reasons for your answer.

2 Read lines 140–51. How do the rhyme and the imagery reveal Helena's feelings?

	And to that place the sharp Athenian law
	Cannot pursue us. If thou lov'st me, then
	Steal forth thy father's house tomorrow night,
	And in the wood, a league without the town,
	(Where I did meet thee once with Helena 130
	To do observance to a morn of May)
	There will I stay for thee.
Hermia	My good Lysander,
	I swear to thee by Cupid's strongest bow,
	By his best arrow with the golden head,
	By all the vows that ever men have broke, 135
	(In number more than ever women spoke),
	In that same place thou hast appointed me,
	Tomorrow truly will I meet with thee.
Lysander	Keep promise, love. Look, here comes Helena.

Enter Helena.

Hermia	God speed fair Helena. Whither away? 140
Helena	Call you me fair? That fair again unsay.
	Demetrius loves your fair. O happy fair!
	Your eyes are lode-stars, and your tongue's sweet air
	More tuneable than lark to shepherd's ear
	When wheat is green, when hawthorn buds appear. 145
	Sickness is catching. O were favour so,
	Yours would I catch, fair Hermia, ere I go.
	My ear should catch your voice, my eye your eye,
	My tongue should catch your tongue's sweet melody.
	O, teach me how you look, and with what art 150
	You sway the motion of Demetrius' heart.
Hermia	I frown upon him, yet he loves me still.
Helena	O that your frowns would teach my smiles such skill.
Hermia	I give him curses, yet he gives me love.
Helena	O that my prayers could such affection move. 155
Hermia	The more I hate, the more he follows me.
Helena	The more I love, the more he hateth me.
Hermia	His folly, Helena, is none of mine.
Helena	None but your beauty. Would that fault were mine.
Hermia	Take comfort. He no more shall see my face, 160
	Lysander and myself will fly this place.
Lysander	Helen, to you our minds we will unfold.
	Tomorrow night, when Phoebe doth behold
	Her silver visage in the watery glass,
	Decking with liquid pearl the bladed grass 165
	(A time that lovers' flights doth still conceal)
	Through Athens' gates have we devised to steal.

128 Steal forth: creep out of
129 a league: about 3 miles
131 to do observance: to celebrate
131 a morn of May: May Day
132 stay: wait
133 Cupid: the god of love (son of Venus, the goddess of love) whose arrows made people fall in love
140 God speed: God go with you
140 fair: lovely
140 Whither away?: where are you off to?
141 unsay: take back
143 lode-stars: guiding stars
143 your tongue's sweet air: your voice
144 tuneable: tuneful
146 favour: beauty and manners
150 art: skill
151 sway the motion: affect the direction of
158 folly: foolish behaviour
158 none of mine: not my fault
161 will fly this place: are going to run away from Athens
163 Phoebe: another name for the goddess of the moon
164 visage: face
164 watery glass: mirror-like water
165 Decking: decorating
165 liquid pearl: dew
166 still: always
167 devised to steal: planned to slip away

Hermia about to kiss Lysander goodbye. Helena sitting on the ground.
This is a different production (2008) from the one in all the other photographs so far (2012). What different impressions do the costumes give of these three young people in the different productions?

Hermia	And in the wood, where often you and I	
	Upon faint primrose-beds were wont to lie,	
	Emptying our bosoms of their counsel sweet,	170
	There my Lysander and myself shall meet,	
	And thence from Athens turn away our eyes	
	To seek new friends and strange companions.	
	Farewell sweet playfellow, pray thou for us,	
	And good luck grant thee thy Demetrius.	175
	Keep word Lysander, we must starve our sight	
	From lovers' food till morrow deep midnight.	
Lysander	I will my Hermia. *Hermia exits.*	
	Helena, adieu.	
	As you on him, Demetrius dote on you! *He exits.*	
Helena	How happy some o'er other some can be!	180
	Through Athens I am thought as fair as she.	
	But what of that? Demetrius thinks not so.	
	He will not know what all but he do know,	
	And as he errs, doting on Hermia's eyes,	
	So I, admiring of his qualities.	185
	Love looks not with the eyes, but with the mind,	
	And therefore is winged Cupid painted blind.	
	For, ere Demetrius looked on Hermia's eyne,	
	He hailed down oaths that he was only mine,	
	And when this hail some heat from Hermia felt,	190
	So he dissolved, and showers of oaths did melt.	
	I will go tell him of fair Hermia's flight.	
	Then to the wood will he tomorrow night	
	Pursue her; and for this intelligence,	
	If I have thanks, it is a dear expense.	195
	But herein mean I to enrich my pain,	
	To have his sight thither, and back again. *She exits.*	

169 were wont to lie: often lay
170 emptying … counsel sweet: telling each other everything
172 thence: from there
173 strange: as yet unknown

176 Keep word: don't break your promise

180 How happy … can be!: some people are given more happiness than others

184 errs: goes astray
185 So I: I also go astray
188 eyne: eyes
194 intelligence: information
195 it is a dear expense: I'll pay a high price for it (because he'll chase Hermia)
196 herein: here's how
196 mean I: I intend
196 enrich: make even greater
197 To have his sight: to be able to look on him
197 thither: there

These questions are about all of Act 1 Scene 1.

3 How do the words used by Hermia, Egeus and Theseus show an audience how daughters were treated by their parents?

4 How would you advise an actor playing Hermia in this scene to behave as she faces Theseus, her father and Demetrius? How could her behaviour change when talking to Lysander and Hermia later in the scene?

5 At the time Shakespeare was writing most wealthy families would have arranged marriages for their children. How might an audience at the time have felt about the way Hermia speaks to her father and her decision to run away with Lysander?

6 This scene has recurring metaphors of love, sight and nature. How are these developed during the scene? How do they help us understand the themes of the play?

7 What does an audience learn about Hippolyta, Hermia and Helena from this scene?

Amateur actors

In Shakespeare's time, skilled workmen like Bottom and the others had to belong to a guild in order to work in their trade. A guild was an organisation of workers. There was a guild for each trade, such as weaving (Bottom) or carpentry (Quince). In medieval times it was traditional for guilds to put on religious-themed plays at certain times of year. This habit had more or less died out in Shakespeare's time. Other groups also put on amateur plays – for example the universities and the law schools.

Act 1 Scene 2

Enter Quince (the carpenter), Snug (the joiner), Bottom (the weaver), Flute (the bellows mender), Snout (the tinker), and Starveling (the tailor).

Quince	Is all our company here?
Bottom	You were best to call them generally, man by man, according to the scrip.
Quince	Here is the scroll of every man's name, which is thought fit through all Athens, to play in our interlude **5** before the Duke and the Duchess, on his wedding day at night.
Bottom	First, good Peter Quince, say what the play treats on, then read the names of the actors, and so grow to a point. **10**
Quince	Marry, our play is, *The most lamentable comedy, and most cruel death of Pyramus and Thisbe.*
Bottom	A very good piece of work, I assure you, and a merry. Now, call forth your actors by the scroll. Masters, spread yourselves. **15**
Quince	Answer as I call you. Nick Bottom, the weaver.
Bottom	Ready. Name what part I am for, and proceed.
Quince	You, Nick Bottom, are set down for Pyramus.
Bottom	What is Pyramus? A lover, or a tyrant?
Quince	A lover that kills himself, most gallantly, for love. **20**
Bottom	That will ask some tears in the true performing of it. If I do it, let the audience look to their eyes. I will move storms; I will condole in some measure. To the rest — yet my chief humour is for a tyrant. I could play Ercles rarely, or a part to tear a cat in. **25**

> The raging rocks
> And shivering shocks
> Shall break the locks
> Of prison gates.
> And Phibbus' car **30**
> Shall shine from far
> And make and mar
> The foolish Fates.

	This was lofty. Now, name the rest of the players. This **34** is Ercles' vein, a tyrant's vein. A lover is more condoling.
Quince	Francis Flute, the bellows-mender.
Flute	Here, Peter Quince.
Quince	Flute, you must take Thisbe on you.
Flute	What is Thisbe? A wandering knight?

1 **company:** group of actors

2 **generally:** he means 'severally' (one at a time: he uses many malapropisms – words used wrongly)

3 **scrip:** list

5 **interlude:** short play

6 **before:** in front of

8 **treats on:** is about

9–10 **grow to a point:** reach your summing-up

11 **Marry:** 'by the Virgin Mary', used at the start of a sentence for emphasis as 'well' is now

11 **lamentable:** sad

12 **Pyramus and Thisbe:** tragic lovers in a famous story

15 **spread yourselves:** spread out

21 **ask:** call for

22 **look to their eyes:** be prepared to be moved to tears

23 **condole:** show great sorrow

24 **my chief humour is for:** I'd rather play

24 **Ercles:** the Greek hero Hercules

25 **rarely:** amazingly well

25 **to tear a cat in:** for ranting and raging

30 **Phibbus' car:** the chariot of Phoebus Apollo, the Greek sun god

32 **mar:** ruin

33 **Fates:** three women in the myths of many cultures who controlled human life

34 **lofty:** impressive, grand

35 **vein:** way of carrying on

39 **wandering knight:** knight travelling in search of adventure

Boys and men as women

In Shakespeare's time, women were not allowed to act in public theatres. Boys and men played all the parts. An acting company usually included experienced actors and boys learning their trade as apprentices. Leading female roles, such as Titania, Helena and Hermia in *A Midsummer Night's Dream*, were played by boy actors whose voices had not yet broken. Some older men specialised in playing older women; sometimes seriously, sometimes in a comic style.

Bottom
How is Bottom suggesting he might play Thisbe?

Quince	It is the lady that Pyramus must love.	**40**
Flute	Nay, faith, let not me play a woman. I have a beard coming.	
Quince	That's all one. You shall play it in a mask, and you may speak as small as you will.	
Bottom	An I may hide my face, let me play Thisbe too. I'll speak in a monstrous little voice. "Thisne, Thisne! " — "Ah, Pyramus, my lover dear, thy Thisbe dear, and lady dear."	**46**
Quince	No, no, you must play Pyramus — and Flute, you Thisbe.	
Bottom	Well, proceed.	
Quince	Robin Starveling, the tailor.	**50**
Starveling	Here, Peter Quince.	
Quince	Robin Starveling, you must play Thisbe's mother. — Tom Snout, the tinker.	
Snout	Here, Peter Quince.	
Quince	You, Pyramus' father; myself, Thisbe's father. Snug, the joiner, you, the lion's part. And I hope here is a play fitted.	**55**
Snug	Have you the lion's part written? Pray you, if it be, give it me, for I am slow of study.	
Quince	You may do it extempore, for it is nothing but roaring.	**60**
Bottom	Let me play the lion too. I will roar, that I will do any man's heart good to hear me. I will roar, that I will make the Duke say, "Let him roar again, let him roar again."	
Quince	If you should do it too terribly, you would fright the Duchess and the ladies, that they would shriek, and that were enough to hang us all.	**65**
Bottom	But I will aggravate my voice so, that I will roar you as gently as any sucking dove; I will roar you an 'twere any nightingale.	
Quince	You can play no part but Pyramus, for Pyramus is a sweet-faced man, a proper man, as one shall see in a summer's day, a most lovely gentleman-like man. Therefore you must needs play Pyramus.	**70**
Bottom	Well, I will undertake it. What beard were I best to play it in?	**75**
Quince	Why, what you will.	
Bottom	I will discharge it in either your straw-colour beard, your orange-tawny beard, your purple-in-grain beard, or your French-crown-colour beard, your perfect yellow.	
Quince	Some of your French-crowns have no hair at all, and then you will play bare-faced. But masters, here are	**80**

43 that's all one: it doesn't matter
43 you may: you need to
44 as small as you will: as high-pitched as you can
45 An: if

57 fitted: well-cast

59 of study: to learn things
60 extempore: without a script

67 aggravate: he means 'moderate'
68 sucking dove: he confuses two phrases for gentleness: 'sitting dove' and 'sucking lamb'
68 an 'twere: as if it was

76 what you will: it's up to you
77 discharge: play
78 purple-in-grain: deep red
79 French-crown-colour: golden or yellow
80 Some of … at all: Some Frenchmen are bald (refers to syphilis, then called 'the French disease', which caused baldness)

From left to right: Flute (Thisbe), Bottom (Pyramus), Quince (standing on a stool), Starveling, and Snout; Quince is speaking lines 82–5.

How do the actors' expressions show how their characters feel about their parts in the play?

your parts. *[Handing out scripts.]* And I am to entreat
you, request you, and desire you, to con them by
tomorrow night, and meet me in the palace wood, a
mile without the town, by moonlight. There will we **85**
rehearse, I pray you, fail me not.

Bottom   We will meet, and there we may rehearse most
obscenely and courageously. Take pains. Be perfect.
Adieu.

Quince   At the Duke's Oak we meet.   **90**

Bottom   Enough. Hold or cut bow-strings.

They exit.

83 **con:** learn

85 **without:** outside

88 **obscenely:** he means 'obscurely'
– secretly

88 **take pains:** make an effort

88 **Be perfect:** learn your parts
thoroughly

91 **Hold or cut bow-strings:** keep
your word or be disgraced (an
archer's saying, stand and fight or
give up)

Bottom and clowns

Most acting companies included at least one 'clown'. This was someone
who was good at comic parts. Most clowns added to the part written for
them, probably adding *ad libs* depending on audience reaction. Sometimes
stage directions refer to 'a clown' or 'clowns' (see page 41) instead of listing
the parts played by the comic actors. The workmen in *A Midsummer Night's
Dream* were all clowning, but the main clown part was that of Bottom.

These questions are about all of Act 1 Scene 2.

1   In what ways is the dialogue in this scene different from the way the characters speak in the previous scene? What
impact does this have on the way we see the Mechanicals?

2   Peter Quince and Bottom dominate the dialogue in this scene. If you were directing a performance of the play how would
you advise the actors playing them to speak and move to show what they want to do with their play?

3   At the time Shakespeare was writing, rich and powerful people **often** asked actors to put on plays for special events.
What might an audience at the time have thought about a group of ordinary workers hoping to put on a play for
Theseus and Hippolyta's wedding?

4   How does this scene begin the theme of confusion and things being turned upside down that runs through the play?

5   What does an audience learn about the character of Bottom in this scene? Think about the way he interrupts Quince
and how he tries to take the role of several characters in the play.

These questions ask you to reflect on all of Act 1.

a)   How are words and imagery used in Act 1 to show different emotions such as anger, true love and also comedy?

b)   In Act 1, how important is it for an audience to understand the way in which people from different levels of society
behaved in Shakespeare's time?

c)   How is the theme of true love not running smoothly begun in Act 1? As well as the lovers in Scene 1, think of Scene
2 and the play Bottom and the others are planning.

d)   What does the audience learn about the main characters in Act 1?

e)   What do we learn about the position of women in the Athens of the play in Act 1?

A

What's just happened

- We are in the woods outside Athens – where the powerful Fairies live.
- This is also the wood where Hermia and Lysander arranged to meet, then run away together.
- Helena has told Demetrius about Hermia and Lysander's plan.

Is there anybody who understands everything that is going on?

Puck

In Shakespeare's time, Puck was a well-known figure in folk tales. The audience would have known many stories and songs about him. He was not a tiny winged creature like fairies in modern stories; he was a mischievous shape-changer. He could turn himself into other things, such as a stool, an animal, or a ghost. He used this skill to play tricks on people, like the woman who falls off her stool. Although there were stories about Puck being helpful, most stories were about tricks, some harmless, some not. Shakespeare's Puck plays tricks, but the audience is clearly meant to like him.

Puck, from three different productions: 2016 (top), 2008 (left) and 2012 (right); this book mostly follows the 2008 and 2012 productions.
What are the main similarities and differences? Which Puck do you think is the most interesting?

B

C

Act 2 Scene 1

Enter a Fairy at one door and Puck at another.

Puck	How now spirit, whither wander you?
Fairy	Over hill, over dale,
	Thorough bush, thorough briar,
	Over park, over pale,
	Thorough flood, thorough fire, **5**
	I do wander everywhere,
	Swifter than the moon's sphere;
	And I serve the Fairy Queen,
	To dew her orbs upon the green.
	I must go seek some dewdrops here **10**
	And hang a pearl in every cowslip's ear.
	Farewell thou lob of spirits, I'll be gone,
	Our Queen and all her elves come here anon.
Puck	The king doth keep his revels here tonight.
	Take heed the Queen come not within his sight, **15**
	For Oberon is passing fell and wrath,
	Because that she, as her attendant, hath
	A lovely boy stolen from an Indian king.
	She never had so sweet a changeling
	And jealous Oberon would have the child **20**
	Knight of his train, to trace the forests wild.
	But she, perforce, withholds the lovèd boy,
	Crowns him with flowers, and makes him all her joy.
	And now they never meet in grove or green,
	By fountain clear, or spangled starlight sheen, **25**
	But they do square, that all their elves for fear
	Creep into acorn-cups and hide them there.
Fairy	Either I mistake your shape and making quite,
	Or else you are that shrewd and knavish sprite
	Called Robin Goodfellow. Are not you he **30**
	That frights the maidens of the villag'ry?
Puck	Thou speak'st aright,
	I am that merry wand'rer of the night.
	I jest to Oberon and make him smile
	When I a fat and bean-fed horse beguile, **35**
	Neighing in likeness of a filly foal.
	The wisest aunt telling the saddest tale,
	Sometime for three-foot stool mistaketh me,
	Then slip I from her bum, down topples she,
	And "tailor" cries, and falls into a cough. **40**
	But room, fairy! Here comes Oberon.
Fairy	And here my mistress. Would that he were gone!

3 **thorough:** through

4 **park:** area of countryside fenced for private hunting

4 **pale:** fence

7 **sphere:** orbit

9 **orbs upon the green:** fairy rings (dark circles) in the grass

12 **thou lob of spirits:** you loutish spirit

13 **anon:** any minute now

14 **doth keep his revels:** is bringing his court

15 **take heed:** make sure

16 **passing fell:** very bitter

16 **wrath:** angry

19 **changeling:** a human child swapped at birth by fairies

21 **Knight of his train:** one of his more important followers

21 **trace:** wander through

22 **perforce:** forcibly

25 **fountain:** spring where a river or stream begins

25 **spangled starlight sheen:** in the bright, glittering starlight

26 **square:** quarrel

28 **making:** physical appearance

28 **quite:** entirely

29 **shrewd:** malicious, spiteful

29 **knavish:** deceitful

31 **villag'ry:** villagers

34 **jest to:** tell jokes to

35 **beguile:** trick

36 **in likeness of a filly foal:** just like a young female horse

37 **aunt:** old woman

40 **"tailor":** 'bum' ('tail' was another word for 'bum')

41 **room:** get out of the way

Titania and Oberon
What does the actors' body language suggest about the relationship between Titania and Oberon?

The weather

The weather had a big effect on people's lives. A wet summer meant a bad harvest, and poorer people would go hungry – there were famines in parts of England in the 1590s, the decade Shakespeare wrote *A Midsummer Night's Dream*. Many people were superstitious about the weather, believing witches or fairies had the power to change it.

Enter Oberon with his attendants at one door,
and Titania with her attendants at another.

Oberon Ill met by moonlight, proud Titania.

Titania What, jealous Oberon? Fairies skip hence:
I have forsworn his bed and company.　　45

Oberon Tarry, rash wanton. Am not I thy lord?

Titania Then I must be thy lady. Why art thou here,
Come from the farthest step of India?
But that, forsooth, the bouncing Amazon,
Your buskined mistress and your warrior love,　　50
To Theseus must be wedded; and you come
To give their bed joy and prosperity?

Oberon How canst thou thus, for shame Titania,
Glance at my credit with Hippolyta,
Knowing I know thy love to Theseus?　　55

Titania These are the forgeries of jealousy.
And never, since the middle summer's spring,
Met we on hill, in dale, forest, or mead,
But with thy brawls thou hast disturbed our sport.
Therefore the winds, piping to us in vain,　　60
As in revenge, have sucked up from the sea
Contagious fogs, which falling in the land,
Hath every petty river made so proud
That they have overborne their continents.
The fold stands empty in the drownèd field,　　65
And crows are fatted with the murrion flock.
The human mortals want their winter cheer,
No night is now with hymn or carol blest.
Therefore the moon (the governess of floods)
Pale in her anger, washes all the air,　　70
That rheumatic diseases do abound.
And through this distemperature we see
The seasons alter. The spring, the summer,
The childing autumn, angry winter, change
Their wonted liveries, and the mazèd world　　75
By their increase, now knows not which is which.
And this same progeny of evils comes
From our debate, from our dissension.
We are their parents and original.

Oberon Do you amend it then, it lies in you.　　80
Why should Titania cross her Oberon?
I do but beg a little changeling boy,
To be my henchman.

Titania 　　　　　　　　Set your heart at rest,
The Fairy Land buys not the child of me.

45	**forsworn:** sworn to avoid
46	**tarry:** wait
46	**rash wanton:** headstrong, unfaithful woman
46	**thy lord:** your husband
47	**thy lady:** your wife
49	**the bouncing Amazon:** Hippolyta
50	**buskined:** wearing buskins – a kind of boot
54	**Glance at my credit with:** make accusations to me about
56	**the forgeries of jealousy:** jealous imaginings
57	**spring:** beginning
58	**mead:** grassy field
59	**brawls:** quarrelling
62	**Contagious:** disease-spreading
63	**petty:** small
64	**overborne their continents:** overflowed
65	**fold:** sheep enclosure
66	**are fatted with:** eat
66	**murrion flock:** diseased sheep
67	**want:** have to do without
69	**Therefore:** because of our dispute
69	**governess of floods:** ruler of the tides
72	**distemperature:** disordered weather
74	**childing:** fertile
75	**wonted liveries:** usual uniform
75	**mazèd:** confused
76	**their increase:** what they produce
77	**this same progeny of evils:** all these bad consequences
78	**dissension:** disagreement
79	**original:** where they come from
80	**Do you amend it:** you put it right

Changelings

In Shakespeare's time, many people believed in fairies, just as they believed in witches. To them, fairies were magical creatures that could change shape and size and could interact with humans without being seen by them. They were said to sometimes swap an ugly baby for a pretty human one. The swapped babies were called 'changelings'.

Titania and the Indian Boy, line 90
Shakespeare does not have a stage direction bringing the boy on stage. Why might the director of this production have decided to bring him on?

	His mother was a votress of my order,	85
	And, in the spicèd Indian air, by night	
	Full often hath she gossiped by my side.	
	But she, being mortal, of that boy did die,	
	And for her sake do I rear up her boy,	
	And for her sake I will not part with him.	90
Oberon	How long within this wood intend you stay?	
Titania	Perchance till after Theseus' wedding day.	
	If you will patiently dance in our round	
	And see our moonlight revels, go with us.	
	If not, shun me and I will spare your haunts.	95
Oberon	Give me that boy, and I will go with thee.	
Titania	Not for thy fairy kingdom. Fairies, away!	
	We shall chide downright if I longer stay.	

Exit Titania and her attendants.

Oberon	Well, go thy way. Thou shalt not from this grove	
	Till I torment thee for this injury.	100
	My gentle Puck come hither. Thou rememb'rest	
	Since once I sat upon a promontory	
	And heard a mermaid, on a dolphin's back,	
	Uttering such dulcet and harmonious breath	
	That the rude sea grew civil at her song,	105
	And certain stars shot madly from their spheres	
	To hear the sea-maid's music?	
Puck	I remember.	
Oberon	That very time I saw (but thou couldst not)	
	Flying between the cold moon and the earth,	
	Cupid all armed. A certain aim he took	110
	At a fair vestal, thronèd by the west.	
	Yet marked I where the bolt of Cupid fell.	
	It fell upon a little western flower,	
	Before, milk-white, now purple with love's wound,	
	And maidens call it love-in-idleness.	115
	Fetch me that flower, the herb I showed thee once.	
	The juice of it on sleeping eye-lids laid	
	Will make or man or woman madly dote	
	Upon the next live creature that it sees.	
Puck	I'll put a girdle round about the earth	120
	In forty minutes. *He exits.*	
Oberon	Having once this juice,	
	I'll watch Titania when she is asleep,	
	And drop the liquor of it in her eyes.	
	The next thing then she waking looks upon,	
	(Be it on lion, bear, or wolf, or bull,	125
	On meddling monkey, or on busy ape)	

85 **a votress:** a priestess

87 **Full often:** many times
88 **of that boy did die:** died giving birth to the boy

92 **Perchance:** probably
93 **patiently:** calmly

95 **shun:** avoid
95 **spare your haunts:** keep out of your way

98 **chide downright:** fall out completely
99 **go thy way:** do as you please
99 **from:** leave

102 **Since:** when
102 **promontory:** headland
104 **Uttering such … breath:** singing so beautifully
105 **rude:** rough
105 **civil:** gentle
106 **spheres:** orbits

110 **all:** fully
110 **certain:** sure
111 **vestal:** virgin
111 **thronèd by:** ruling in
112 **marked I:** I noticed
112 **the bolt:** the arrow
115 **love-in-idleness:** a flower, pansy, also called 'heartsease'
118 **or … or:** either … or
118–9 **madly dote Upon:** fall madly in love with
120 **girdle:** belt
120 **round about:** around
121 **Having once:** When I have

Demetrius and Helena
Is this photograph more likely to have been taken at line 133, 139, 154 or 169?

1 What do Demetrius's words
suggest about his character?

28

She shall pursue it with the soul of love.
And ere I take this charm from off her sight,
(As I can take it with another herb)
I'll make her render up her page to me. —   130
But who comes here? I am invisible,
And I will overhear their conference.

Enter Demetrius, then Helena following him.

Demetrius	I love thee not, therefore pursue me not.
	Where is Lysander and fair Hermia?
	The one I'll stay, the other stayeth me. 135
	Thou told'st me they were stol'n unto this wood,
	And here am I, and wood within this wood
	Because I cannot meet my Hermia.
	Hence, get thee gone, and follow me no more.
Helena	You draw me, you hard-hearted adamant, 140
	But yet you draw not iron, for my heart
	Is true as steel. Leave you your power to draw,
	And I shall have no power to follow you.
Demetrius	Do I entice you? Do I speak you fair?
	Or, rather, do I not in plainest truth 145
	Tell you, I do not, nor I cannot love you?
Helena	And even for that do I love thee the more.
	I am your spaniel, and, Demetrius,
	The more you beat me, I will fawn on you.
	Use me but as your spaniel, spurn me, strike me, 150
	Neglect me, lose me; only give me leave
	(Unworthy as I am) to follow you.
Demetrius	Tempt not too much the hatred of my spirit,
	For I am sick when I do look on thee.
Helena	And I am sick when I look not on you. 155
Demetrius	You do impeach your modesty too much,
	To leave the city and commit yourself
	Into the hands of one that loves you not,
	To trust the opportunity of night,
	And the ill counsel of a desert place, 160
	With the rich worth of your virginity.
Helena	Your virtue is my privilege. For that
	It is not night when I do see your face,
	Therefore I think I am not in the night.
	Nor doth this wood lack worlds of company, 165
	For you, in my respect, are all the world.
	Then how can it be said I am alone,
	When all the world is here to look on me?
Demetrius	I'll run from thee and hide me in the brakes,
	And leave thee to the mercy of wild beasts. 170

Glossary

127 pursue it … of love: fall madly in love with it
128 ere: before
130 render up: give

132 conference: conversation

135 the one I'll stay: I'll stop one
135 the other stayeth me: the other keeps me here
137 wood: driven to fury
139 Hence: leave here
140 draw me: pull me to you
140 adamant: both a magnet and a very hard metal
142 Leave you: give up

144 speak you fair: talk to you kindly

148 spaniel: a breed of dog famous for being faithful even if ill-treated
149 fawn on: lavish love on
150 Use me but as: treat me just like
150 spurn me: reject or kick
151 leave: permission
153 tempt not … my spirit: don't push your luck

156 You do impeach … much: you're putting your reputation to too great a test

160 the ill counsel of a desert place: in a lonely place where you can't call for help
162 Your virtue … privilege: I'm safe with you, you are a good man
162 For that: because
166 in my respect: to me

169 brakes: bushes

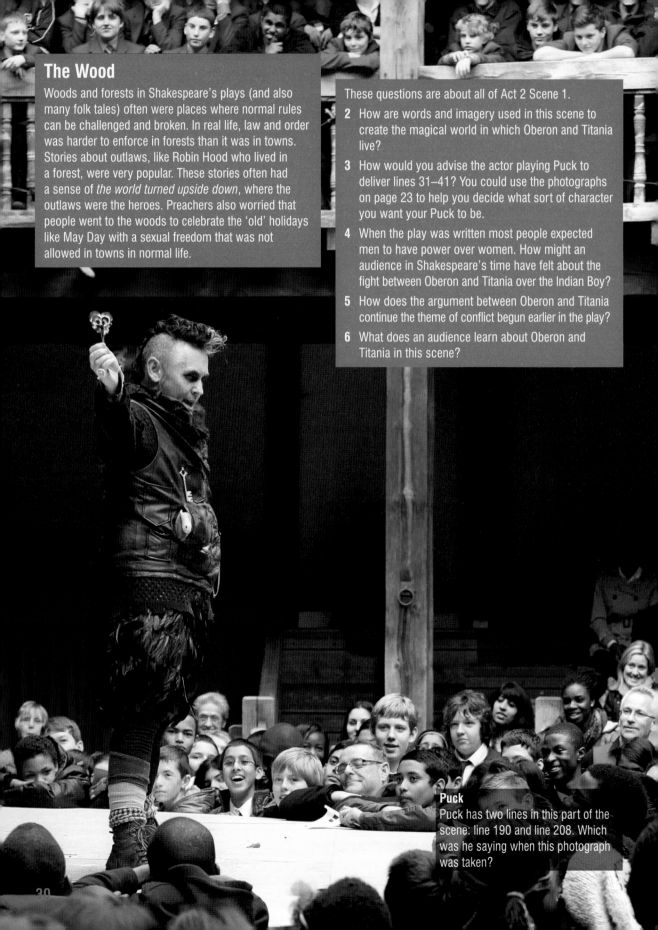

The Wood

Woods and forests in Shakespeare's plays (and also many folk tales) often were places where normal rules can be challenged and broken. In real life, law and order was harder to enforce in forests than it was in towns. Stories about outlaws, like Robin Hood who lived in a forest, were very popular. These stories often had a sense of *the world turned upside down*, where the outlaws were the heroes. Preachers also worried that people went to the woods to celebrate the 'old' holidays like May Day with a sexual freedom that was not allowed in towns in normal life.

These questions are about all of Act 2 Scene 1.

2   How are words and imagery used in this scene to create the magical world in which Oberon and Titania live?

3   How would you advise the actor playing Puck to deliver lines 31–41? You could use the photographs on page 23 to help you decide what sort of character you want your Puck to be.

4   When the play was written most people expected men to have power over women. How might an audience in Shakespeare's time have felt about the fight between Oberon and Titania over the Indian Boy?

5   How does the argument between Oberon and Titania continue the theme of conflict begun earlier in the play?

6   What does an audience learn about Oberon and Titania in this scene?

Puck
Puck has two lines in this part of the scene: line 190 and line 208. Which was he saying when this photograph was taken?

Helena	The wildest hath not such a heart as you.
	Run when you will, the story shall be changed:
	Apollo flies, and Daphne holds the chase;
	The dove pursues the griffin; the mild hind
	Makes speed to catch the tiger. Bootless speed,	175
	When cowardice pursues and valour flies.
Demetrius	I will not stay thy questions. Let me go!
	Or if thou follow me, do not believe
	But I shall do thee mischief in the wood.
Helena	Ay, in the temple, in the town, the field,	180
	You do me mischief. Fie, Demetrius,
	Your wrongs do set a scandal on my sex.
	We cannot fight for love, as men may do,
	We should be wooed and were not made to woo.

Demetrius exits.

I'll follow thee, and make a heaven of hell,   185
To die upon the hand I love so well.   *She exits.*

| Oberon | Fare thee well nymph. Ere he do leave this grove, |
| | Thou shalt fly him, and he shall seek thy love. |

Enter Puck.

Hast thou the flower there? Welcome, wanderer.

Puck	Ay, there it is.
Oberon	I pray thee give it me. 190
	I know a bank where the wild thyme blows,
	Where oxlips and the nodding violet grows,
	Quite over-canopied with luscious woodbine,
	With sweet musk-roses and with eglantine.
	There sleeps Titania, sometime of the night, 195
	Lulled in these flowers with dances and delight.
	And with the juice of this I'll streak her eyes,
	And make her full of hateful fantasies.

[Giving him some of the flower.]

Take thou some of it, and seek through this grove;
A sweet Athenian lady is in love   200
With a disdainful youth. Anoint his eyes,
But do it when the next thing he espies
May be the lady. Thou shalt know the man
By the Athenian garments he hath on.
Effect it with some care, that he may prove   205
More fond on her than she upon her love.
And look thou meet me ere the first cock crow.

| Puck | Fear not my lord, your servant shall do so. |

They exit.

173 Apollo flies: in Greek myths, the god Apollo chased Daphne
174 griffin: fierce mythical animal: part lion, part eagle
174 hind: female deer
175 Bootless: pointless
176 valour: bravery
177 stay: wait for
178–9 do not believe But: you had better believe
179 do thee mischief: harm you
181 Fie: shame on you!
182 Your wrongs … my sex: you force me to behave in a way that disgraces women
186 to die upon: to be killed by
187 nymph: lovely girl (nymphs were beautiful spirits in Greek myths)
187 grove: wood
191 a bank: a sheltered, sloping, piece of land
191 blows: blooms
193 Quite over-canopied with: with a thick roof of
193 woodbine: honeysuckle
194 eglantine: a wild rose
195 sometime of: for part of
196 Lulled: sent to sleep in
196 with: by
197 streak: smear
198 hateful fantasies: unpleasant imaginings
201 disdainful: scornful
202 espies: sees
205 Effect: do
205 that: so that
206 fond on: infatuated with

Oberon drugs Titania, who is sleeping next to the Indian Boy, lines 15–21. How does what the audience sees of Titania contrast with what Oberon says?

1 As Oberon pours the juice into Titania's eyes, what do his words tell the audience about his character?

Act 2 Scene 2

Enter Titania and her attendant Fairies.

Titania	Come, now a roundel and a fairy song.
	Sing me now asleep,
	Then to your offices, and let me rest.

She lies down, the Fairies sing.

All   *You spotted snakes with double tongue,*
Thorny hedgehogs be not seen;   **5**
Newts and blind-worms do no wrong,
Come not near our Fairy Queen.
Philomel, with melody,
Sing in our sweet lullaby.
Lulla lulla lullaby, lulla lulla lullaby,   **10**
Never harm, nor spell nor charm,
Come our lovely lady nigh;
So, good night, with lullaby.

Titania sleeps.

Second Fairy   Hence away, now all is well.   *The Fairies exit.*

Enter Oberon.

Oberon   *[Squeezing the juice of the flower in Titania's eyes.]*
What thou seest when thou dost wake,   **15**
Do it for thy true-love take.
Love and languish for his sake.
Be it ounce, or cat, or bear,
In thy eye that shall appear
When thou wak'st, it is thy dear.   **20**
Wake when some vile thing is near.   *He exits.*

Enter Lysander and Hermia.

Lysander   Fair love, you faint with wand'ring in the wood,
And to speak troth, I have forgot our way.
We'll rest us Hermia, if you think it good,
And tarry for the comfort of the day.   **25**

Hermia   Be it so Lysander. Find you out a bed,
For I upon this bank will rest my head.

Lysander   One turf shall serve as pillow for us both,
One heart, one bed, two bosoms, and one troth.

Hermia   Nay, good Lysander, for my sake, my dear,   **30**
Lie further off yet, do not lie so near.

Lysander   O, take the sense, sweet, of my innocence.
Love takes the meaning in love's conference.
I mean that my heart unto yours is knit,
So that but one heart we can make of it.   **35**

---

1   **roundel:** dance in a circle

3   **offices:** jobs

4   **double:** forked

6   **blind-worms:** adders

8   **Philomel:** the nightingale

12   **nigh:** near

14   **Hence away:** Let's go

17   **languish:** pine away
18   **ounce:** lynx

23   **to speak troth:** to tell you the truth
24   **think it good:** agree
25   **tarry:** wait
25   **comfort of the day:** encouragement of daylight
26   **Find you out:** find yourself

29   **bosoms:** hearts
29   **troth:** faithful promise of love

32   **take the sense:** understand
33   **Love takes … conference:** lovers instinctively understand each other

Puck drugging Lysander, lines 65–8.
In this production, Puck used his fairy magic to remove Lysander's eyeballs, drug him, then put them back. Why might the director have added this?

	Two bosoms interchainèd with an oath,	
	So then two bosoms and a single troth.	
	Then by your side no bed-room me deny,	
	For lying so, Hermia, I do not lie.	
Hermia	Lysander riddles very prettily.	40
	Now much beshrew my manners and my pride,	
	If Hermia meant to say Lysander lied.	
	But, gentle friend, for love and courtesy	
	Lie further off, in human modesty.	
	Such separation, as may well be said	45
	Becomes a virtuous bachelor and a maid,	
	So far be distant, and, good night, sweet friend.	
	Thy love ne'er alter till thy sweet life end.	
Lysander	Amen, amen, to that fair prayer, say I,	
	And then end life when I end loyalty!	50
	Here is my bed, sleep give thee all his rest.	
Hermia	With half that wish the wisher's eyes be pressed!	

They sleep.

Enter Puck.

Puck	Through the forest have I gone,	
	But Athenian found I none,	
	On whose eyes I might approve	55
	This flower's force in stirring love.	
	Night and silence. — Who is here?	
	Weeds of Athens he doth wear.	
	This is he, my master said,	
	Despisèd the Athenian maid.	60
	And here the maiden, sleeping sound,	
	On the dank and dirty ground.	
	Pretty soul, she durst not lie	
	Near this lack-love, this kill-courtesy.	

[Squeezing the juice of the flower on Lysander's eyes.]

	Churl, upon thy eyes I throw	65
	All the power this charm doth owe.	
	When thou wak'st, let love forbid	
	Sleep his seat on thy eyelid.	
	So awake when I am gone,	
	For I must now to Oberon.	*He exits.* 70

Enter Demetrius running, chased by Helena.

Helena	Stay, though thou kill me, sweet Demetrius.	
Demetrius	I charge thee, hence, and do not haunt me thus.	
Helena	O wilt thou darkling leave me? Do not so.	
Demetrius	Stay, on thy peril, I alone will go.	*Exit Demetrius.*

---

39 lie: mislead you (pun on lying down)

40 prettily: cleverly, neatly

41 much beshrew: shame on

46 Becomes: is suitable between

47 So far be distant: that's about the right distance

50 And then … loyalty: may I die if I'm ever disloyal to you

52 With half … be pressed!: I share the restful sleep you wish me with you

55 approve: test

58 Weeds: clothes

62 dank: damp

63 durst not: doesn't dare

65 churl: ill-mannered villain

66 owe: possess

67–8 let love forbid … eyelid: you'll be so in love you can't sleep

72 charge thee: order you

72 haunt: follow me everywhere

73 darkling: in the dark

Lysander and Helena
Study the actors' body language and expressions. Which of these lines is Lysander likely to be speaking: lines 85–6, lines 94–5, or line 99?

Helena	O, I am out of breath in this fond chase! 75
	The more my prayer, the lesser is my grace.
	Happy is Hermia, wheresoe'er she lies,
	For she hath blessèd and attractive eyes.
	How came her eyes so bright? Not with salt tears.
	If so, my eyes are oftener washed than hers. 80
	No, no, I am as ugly as a bear,
	For beasts that meet me run away for fear.
	But who is here? Lysander on the ground?
	Dead or asleep? I see no blood, no wound.
	Lysander, if you live, good sir awake. 85
Lysander	*[Waking.]*
	And run through fire I will for thy sweet sake.
	Transparent Helena! Nature shows art,
	That through thy bosom makes me see thy heart.
	Where is Demetrius? O how fit a word
	Is that vile name to perish on my sword! 90
Helena	Do not say so, Lysander. Say not so.
	What though he love your Hermia? Lord, what though?
	Yet Hermia still loves you. Then be content.
Lysander	Content with Hermia? No, I do repent
	The tedious minutes I with her have spent. 95
	Not Hermia, but Helena I love.
	Who will not change a raven for a dove?
	The will of man is by his reason swayed,
	And reason says you are the worthier maid.
	And touching now the point of human skill, 100
	Reason becomes the marshal to my will,
	And leads me to your eyes, where I o'erlook
	Love's stories written in love's richest book.
Helena	Wherefore was I to this keen mockery born?
	When, at your hands, did I deserve this scorn? 105
	Is't not enough, is't not enough, young man,
	That I did never, no nor never can,
	Deserve a sweet look from Demetrius' eye,
	But you must flout my insufficiency?
	Good troth, you do me wrong, good sooth, you do, 110
	In such disdainful manner me to woo.
	But fare you well. Perforce I must confess
	I thought you lord of more true gentleness.
	O, that a lady of one man refused, 114
	Should of another therefore be abused! *She exits.*
Lysander	She sees not Hermia. Hermia, sleep thou there,
	And never mayst thou come Lysander near.
	For as a surfeit of the sweetest things
	The deepest loathing to the stomach brings,

75 fond: double meaning: 1) infatuated; 2) foolish
76 the more … my grace: the more I beg, the less I get
77 wheresoe'er: wherever

87 Transparent: clear, without deceit
87 nature shows art: nature's very clever

92 Lord, what though?: good God, what does it matter?

97 Who will not … a dove?: Hermia is said to have a dark complexion (raven);Helena a pale one (dove)
98 The will of man: man's wants and desires
100 touching now the point of human skill: now I'm mature enough
101 becomes the marshal to: can control
102 o'erlook: can read
104 Wherefore: why
104 keen: cruel
106 Is't not: isn't it
109 flout my insufficiency: mock my flaws
110 good sooth: indeed
112 Perforce I must confess: though I must say
113 lord of more true gentleness: more of a gentleman
114 of: by
115 abused: mistreated
118 a surfeit: too much of

Hermia wakes up to find herself alone.
Compare this photograph with the one on page 14 (also showing Hermia from this production). How have things changed for her?

Of all be hated, but the most of me!   **120**
And, all my powers, address your love and might,
To honour Helen, and to be her knight.   *He exits.*

Hermia   *[Waking.]* Help me, Lysander, help me! Do thy best
To pluck this crawling serpent from my breast.
Ay me, for pity! What a dream was here!   **125**
Lysander, look how I do quake with fear.
Methought a serpent eat my heart away,
And you sat smiling at his cruel prey.
Lysander! What, removed? Lysander, lord!
What, out of hearing? Gone? No sound, no word?   **130**
Alack, where are you? Speak, an if you hear.
Speak, of all loves! I swoon almost with fear.
No? then I well perceive you are not nigh.
Either death or you I'll find immediately.   *She exits.*

125 Ay me, for pity!: how dreadful!
125 was here: I have had
127 Methought: I imagined
127 eat: ate
128 prey: attack on me
129 removed: gone
131 an if you hear: if you can hear me
132 of all loves: for love's sake
132 swoon: faint
133 I well perceive: I can see

These questions are about all of Act 2 Scene 2.

2 How do Helena's words show her feelings when she hears Lysander now saying he loves her?

3 How would you ask the actor playing Helena to move and speak when she wakes Lysander, who then says he loves her?

4 How should the actor playing Hermia show her feelings when she awakes from a nightmare and finds Lysander has gone?

5 Many people in the audience in Shakespeare's time would have believed in the power of magic. How do you think an audience at the time would have responded to the idea of a magic potion that makes Lysander love Helena instead of Hermia?

6 The play has many transformations (one thing turning into another). How does this scene develop this idea in what happens to Lysander?

These questions ask you to reflect on all of Act 2.

a) How is the mystery and magic in the Forest created through words and imagery in Act 2?

b) What is the significance of this act being set at night?

c) How is the theme of the power of magic developed through the events of Act 2?

d) What does an audience learn about the world of the Forest? What is the same and what is different about it and the world of Athens?

e) What do we learn about the way men view and treat women in this Act?

The Tiring House

In this scene, Quince talks about using one part of the wood as their 'stage' and another as their 'tiring house'. The Tiring House of an Elizabethan theatre was the part behind the stage – what we would call 'backstage'. Actors put on their costumes (their 'attire') here and waited to go on stage. Props, costumes, make-up, wigs, beards and musical instruments were all stored in the tiring house. Lists of the main events of the play (called 'plots') were hung up in the Tiring House, so the actors could follow the play from there. The outside of the Tiring House, the part the audience could see, was the back wall of the stage (see page 4).

What's just happened

- Bottom and the others have agreed to meet in the wood to rehearse their play.
- This is the same part of the wood that Titania is sleeping in.
- Oberon has drugged Titania so that she will love the first creature she sees when she wakes.

How might the workmen be feeling as they meet in the wood to rehearse their play?

Bottom (right) explaining to Snug how they might solve the problem of moonshine, lines 28–30.
What does this speech and the next one (lines 31–3) show about the relationship between Bottom and Quince?

Act 3 Scene 1

Titania remains on the stage asleep. Enter the clowns – Quince, Bottom, Flute, Snout, Snug, and Starveling.

Bottom	Are we all met?
Quince	Pat, pat. And here's a marvellous convenient place for our rehearsal. This green plot shall be our stage, this hawthorn-brake our tiring house, and we will do it in action as we will do it before the Duke. **5**
Bottom	Peter Quince?
Quince	What sayest thou, bully Bottom?
Bottom	There are things in this comedy of Pyramus and Thisbe that will never please. First, Pyramus must draw a sword to kill himself, which the ladies cannot abide. **10** How answer you that?
Snout	By'r lakin, a parlous fear.
Starveling	I believe we must leave the killing out, when all is done.
Bottom	Not a whit, I have a device to make all well. Write me a prologue, and let the prologue seem to say, we will do **15** no harm with our swords, and that Pyramus is not killed indeed. And, for the more better assurance, tell them that I, Pyramus, am not Pyramus, but Bottom the weaver. This will put them out of fear.
Quince	Well, we will have such a prologue. But there is two **20** hard things. That is, to bring the moonlight into a chamber, for, you know, Pyramus and Thisbe meet by moonlight —
Snout	Doth the moon shine that night we play our play?
Bottom	A calendar, a calendar! Look in the almanac. Find out **25** moonshine, find out moonshine.
Quince	*[Looking at a book.]* Yes, it doth shine that night.
Bottom	Why, then may you leave a casement of the great chamber window (where we play) open, and the moon may shine in at the casement. **30**
Quince	Ay, or else one must come in with a bush of thorns and a lantern, and say he comes to disfigure, or to present, the person of Moonshine. Then, there is another thing, we must have a wall in the great chamber; for Pyramus and Thisbe did talk through the chink of a wall. **35**
Snout	You can never bring in a wall. What say you, Bottom?
Bottom	Some man or other must present Wall, and let him have some plaster, or some loam, or some roughcast about him, to signify wall. And let him hold his fingers thus,

2 **Pat, pat:** right on time

4 **hawthorn-brake:** clump of hawthorn bushes

4 **tiring house:** actors' dressing room, behind the stage

7 **bully:** a term of endearment such as 'me old mate'

12 **By'r lakin:** short for 'By Our Lady-kin' (the Virgin Mary), a mild oath

12 **parlous:** perilous

14 **not a whit:** not a bit of it

14 **device:** plan

15 **prologue:** speech to start the play

17 **for the more better assurance:** to be on the safe side

25 **almanac:** calendar

28 **casement:** part of a window

31–2 **bush of … a lantern:** said to be carried by the man in the moon

38 **loam:** clay

38 **roughcast:** a mix of lime, gravel and water used to plaster the outside of walls

39 **thus:** like this

Bottom with an ass's head
Compare this photograph with those of the same actor playing Bottom on pages 18 and 40. How many changes were there to his appearance?

Asides

Asides are lines a character speaks to the audience that the other people on stage cannot hear. Shakespeare uses them to show the audience what the character really thinks or feels. Puck's aside (Act 3 Scene 1, line 46) tells the audience that they can see him but Bottom and the others cannot.

	and through that cranny shall Pyramus and Thisbe whisper.	**40**
Quince	If that may be, then all is well. Come, sit down, every mother's son, and rehearse your parts. Pyramus, you begin. When you have spoken your speech, enter into that brake, and so every one according to his cue.	**45**
	Enter Puck, unseen by the others on stage.	
Puck	*[Aside.]* What hempen homespuns have we swagg'ring here,	
	So near the cradle of the Fairy Queen?	
	What, a play toward? I'll be an auditor,	
	An actor too perhaps, if I see cause.	
Quince	Speak, Pyramus. Thisbe stand forth.	**50**
Pyramus (Bottom)	*Thisbe, the flowers of odious savours sweet, —*	
Quince	Odours — odorous.	
Pyramus (Bottom)	*odours savours sweet,*	
	So hath thy breath, my dearest Thisbe dear.	
	But hark, a voice. Stay thou but here awhile,	**54**
	And by and by I will to thee appear. *Exit Bottom.*	
Puck	A stranger Pyramus than e'er played here. *He exits.*	
Flute	Must I speak now?	
Quince	Ay, marry, must you. For you must understand he goes but to see a noise that he heard, and is to come again.	
Thisbe (Flute)	*Most radiant Pyramus, most lily-white of hue,*	**60**
	Of colour like the red rose on triumphant briar,	
	As true as truest horse, that yet would never tire,	
	I'll meet thee, Pyramus, at Ninny's tomb.	
Quince	"Ninus' tomb," man! Why, you must not speak that yet. That you answer to Pyramus. Pyramus enter, your cue is past, it is, "never tire".	**65**
Flute	O!	
Thisbe (Flute)	*As true as truest horse, that yet would never tire.*	
	Enter Puck, and Bottom with an ass's head.	
Pyramus (Bottom)	*If I were fair, Thisbe, I were only thine.*	
Quince	O monstrous! O strange! We are haunted. Pray, masters, fly, masters! Help!	**70**
	Quince, Bottom, Flute, Snout, Snug, and Starveling run off stage in different directions.	
Puck	I'll follow you. I'll lead you about a round,	
	Through bog, through bush, through brake, through briar.	

Glossary

40 **cranny:** hole, split

42 **If that may be:** if we can do that
43 **rehearse:** speak, practice

45 **brake:** clump of bushes
45 **and so every one:** and you all do that
46 **hempen homespuns:** stupid peasants (only poor people wore the scratchy cloth made from hemp)
47 **cradle:** resting place
48 **toward:** being prepared
48 **I'll be an auditor:** I'll listen
49 **if I see cause:** if I can find a reason
51 **odious:** hateful; he means 'odours' – smells
51 **savours:** smells
55 **by and by:** soon
56 **e'er:** ever
58 **marry:** 'by the Virgin Mary', used at the start of a sentence for emphasis as 'well' is now
58–59 **he goes but:** he's only going to
60 **hue:** colour

63 **Ninny's:** a ninny is a fool; he means 'Ninus' an ancient king

69 **fair:** handsome

72 **a round:** a circular dance

Titania and Bottom
Which line do you think Titania has
just said, line 101 or line 109?

44

Sometime a horse I'll be, sometime a hound,
A hog, a headless bear, sometime a fire,   **75**
And neigh, and bark, and grunt, and roar, and burn,
Like horse, hound, hog, bear, fire, at every turn.

Exit Puck.

Bottom   Why do they run away? This is a knavery of them to
make me afeard.

Enter Snout.

Snout   O Bottom, thou art changed. What do I see on thee?   **80**

Bottom   What do you see? You see an ass-head of your own,
do you?

Exit Snout. Enter Quince.

Quince   Bless thee, Bottom, bless thee. Thou art translated.

Exit Quince.

Bottom   I see their knavery. This is to make an ass of me, to
fright me, if they could. But I will not stir from this   **85**
place, do what they can. I will walk up and down here,
and I will sing, that they shall hear I am not afraid.
[Singing.]   *The ousel cock so black of hue,*
With orange-tawny bill.
The throstle with his note so true,   **90**
The wren with little quill, —

Titania   What angel wakes me from my flowery bed?

Bottom   *The finch, the sparrow and the lark,*
The plain-song cuckoo gray,
Whose note full many a man doth mark, **95**
And dares not answer nay —

Titania   I pray thee, gentle mortal, sing again,
Mine ear is much enamoured of thy note.
So is mine eye enthrallèd to thy shape,
And thy fair virtue's force (perforce) doth move me **100**
On the first view to say, to swear, I love thee.

Bottom   Methinks mistress, you should have little reason for
that. And yet, to say the truth, reason and love keep
little company together now-a-days.

Titania   Thou art as wise as thou art beautiful.   **105**

Bottom   Not so neither. But if I had wit enough to get out of this
wood, I have enough to serve mine own turn.

Titania   Out of this wood do not desire to go,
Thou shalt remain here, whether thou wilt or no.
I am a spirit of no common rate.   **110**
The summer still doth tend upon my state,
And I do love thee. Therefore go with me.

---

75 fire: dancing light that, in the marshes, led travellers astray

83 translated: changed into something else

84 knavery: trick

86 do what they can: no matter what they do

88 ousel cock: male blackbird

89 bill: beak

90 throstle: thrush

91 little quill: high, sharp, song

93 plain-song cuckoo: cuckoo (sounds like cuckold: a man whose wife has been unfaithful) with his simple song

95 mark: hear, notice

96 And dares not answer nay: and can't deny (that he is a cuckold)

98 of thy note: by your singing

99 So: in the same way

99 enthrallèd to: bewitched by

100–1 thy fair virtue's… move me: your good qualities force me

107 to serve mine own turn: for me

109 wilt: want to

110 common rate: ordinary sort

A

B

Bottom, from three different productions: 2016 (left), 2008 (right) and 2012 (below); this book mostly follows 2008 and 2012. What are the main similarities and differences? Which one seems the most interesting?

C

These questions are about all of Act 3 Scene 1.

1 How do Bottom's words to Titania and the Fairies show he is not worried by the strange events that start happening to him? Think about how he talks to each of the Fairies.

2 If you were directing a performance of the play how would you advise the actor playing Bottom to change the way he speaks and moves from when we met him in Act 2?

3 Shakespeare's audiences, like audiences today, were familiar with stories of strange transformations. How might this have helped an audience at the time to accept Bottom's situation?

4 How is the idea of things being turned upside down and transformed developed in this scene?

5 How does Titania's behaviour differ from when we saw her in Act 2? What does that tell us about her?

	I'll give thee fairies to attend on thee,	**113 attend on:** look after
	Peaseblossom, Cobweb, Moth, and Mustardseed!	
	Enter these four Fairies.	

Peaseblossom Ready.

Cobweb And I.

Moth And I.

Mustardseed Where shall we go? **115**

Titania Be kind and courteous to this gentleman.
Hop in his walks and gambol in his eyes,   **117 in his eyes:** for him to see
Feed him with apricocks and dewberries,   **118 apricocks:** apricots
With purple grapes, green figs, and mulberries.   **118 dewberries:** blackberries
And pluck the wings from painted butterflies **120**
To fan the moonbeams from his sleeping eyes.
Nod to him elves, and do him courtesies.   **122 do him courtesies:** greet him politely

Peaseblossom Hail mortal.

Cobweb Hail.

Moth Hail. **125**

Mustardseed Hail.

Bottom I cry your worships mercy heartily. *[To Cobweb.]*   **127 I cry your worships mercy:** he means to use a formal greeting, but begs pardon
I beseech your worship's name.   **128 beseech:** ask

Cobweb Cobweb.

Bottom I shall desire you of more acquaintance, good Master **130**
Cobweb. — Your name, honest gentleman?   **131 kindred:** family (he means mustard to eat)

Peaseblossom Peaseblossom.   **131–2 made my eyes water:** mustard is hot, like chilli

Bottom Peaseblossom, I shall desire of you more acquaintance
too. — Your name, I beseech you, sir?

Mustardseed Mustardseed. **135**

Bottom Mustardseed, I promise you, your kindred had made my
eyes water ere now. I desire your more acquaintance,
good Master Mustardseed.

Titania Come, wait upon him, lead him to my bower.   **139 bower:** resting place
The moon methinks looks with a watery eye, **140**
And when she weeps, weeps every little flower,
Lamenting some enforcèd chastity.   **142 enforcèd chastity:** this could either mean rape, (chastity being forced), or being forced to be chaste
[Bottom makes a load braying noise.]
Tie up my love's tongue, bring him silently.

She exits, the Fairies bring Bottom after her.

Stage directions in the text

Shakespeare often uses one character's lines to tell the other actors what to do. When Oberon says 'Stand close' (line 31), he and Puck know they must hide so they can watch without being seen themselves. Look out for other examples throughout the play.

Puck (with horns) and Oberon, while line 35 was being said.
Who are they looking at? What do their expressions and body language suggest?

Act 3 Scene 2

Enter Oberon.

Oberon	I wonder, if Titania be awaked.

Enter Puck.

	Here comes my messenger. How now, mad spirit?	
	What night-rule now about this haunted grove?	
Puck	My mistress with a monster is in love.	
	Near to her close and consecrated bower,	5
	While she was in her dull and sleeping hour,	
	A crew of patches, rude mechanicals,	
	That work for bread upon Athenian stalls,	
	Were met together to rehearse a play	
	Intended for great Theseus' nuptial day.	10
	The shallowest thick-skin of that barren sort,	
	Who Pyramus presented in their sport,	
	Forsook his scene and entered in a brake.	
	When I did him at this advantage take,	
	An ass's nole I fixèd on his head.	15
	Anon his Thisbe must be answerèd,	
	And forth my mimic comes. When they him spy,	
	And at his sight, away his fellows fly,	
	And at our stamp, here o'er and o'er one falls,	
	He "murder" cries, and help from Athens calls.	20
	I led them on in this distracted fear,	
	And left sweet Pyramus translated there.	
	When in that moment, so it came to pass,	
	Titania waked and straightway loved an ass.	
Oberon	This falls out better than I could devise.	25
	But hast thou yet latched the Athenian's eyes	
	With the love juice, as I did bid thee do?	
Puck	I took him sleeping (that is finished too)	
	And the Athenian woman by his side,	
	That, when he waked, of force she must be eyed.	30

Enter Demetrius and Hermia.

Oberon	Stand close. This is the same Athenian.	
Puck	This is the woman, but not this the man.	

They stand aside.

Demetrius	O why rebuke you him that loves you so?	
	Lay breath so bitter on your bitter foe.	
Hermia	Now I but chide, but I should use thee worse,	35
	For thou, I fear, hast given me cause to curse.	
	If thou hast slain Lysander in his sleep,	
	Being o'er shoes in blood, plunge in the deep,	
	And kill me too.	

What's just happened

- Oberon has drugged Titania.
- Puck (sent to drug Demetrius), drugged Lysander, who (because of the drug) now loves Helena.
- Hermia woke alone, so set off to find Lysander.
- Demetrius is still in the wood.

3 **night-rule:** mischief done in the night

5 **close and consecrated bower:** private sleeping place

7 **patches:** fools

7 **rude mechanicals:** common workmen

8 **work for bread:** earn their living

11 **shallowest thick-skin:** stupidest and most insensitive person

11 **barren sort:** stupid lot

13 **Forsook:** left

13 **scene:** stage

14 **I did him … take:** I took this chance

15 **nole:** head

16 **Anon:** soon

17 **forth:** out

17 **mimic:** actor

19 **at our stamp:** when I stamped

22 **translated:** changed into something else

23 **in that moment:** just then

25 **I could devise:** I could have planned

26 **latched:** covered

30 **of force … eyed:** she had to be the first thing he saw

31 **Stand close:** out of the way, hide

34 **Lay breath … bitter foe:** save bitter words for your enemies

35 **I but chide:** I'm only scolding you

35 **use thee worse:** be harder on you

38 **o'er:** over

Demetrius and Hermia
Why is Hermia so angry?

1 How does Demetrius transform the comparison made by Hermia in line 41?

	It cannot be but thou hast murdered him.	40
	So should a murderer look, so dead, so grim.	
Demetrius	So should the murdered look, and so should I,	
	Pierced through the heart with your stern cruelty.	
	Yet you, the murderer, look as bright, as clear,	
	As yonder Venus in her glimmering sphere.	45
Hermia	What's this to my Lysander? Where is he?	
	Ah, good Demetrius, wilt thou give him me?	
Demetrius	I'd rather give his carcass to my hounds.	
Hermia	Out, dog! Out, cur! Thou driv'st me past the bounds	
	Of maiden's patience. Hast thou slain him then?	50
	Henceforth be never numbered among men.	
Demetrius	You spend your passion on a misprised mood.	
	I am not guilty of Lysander's blood.	
	Nor is he dead for aught that I can tell.	
Hermia	I pray thee tell me then that he is well.	55
Demetrius	And if I could, what should I get therefore?	
Hermia	A privilege, never to see me more.	
	And from thy hated presence part I so,	
	See me no more, whether he be dead or no. *She exits.*	
Demetrius	There is no following her in this fierce vein,	60
	Here therefore for a while I will remain.	

He lies down and sleeps.

Oberon	What hast thou done? Thou hast mistaken quite	
	And laid the love juice on some true-love's sight.	
	About the wood go swifter than the wind,	
	And Helena of Athens look thou find.	65
	By some illusion see thou bring her here.	
	I'll charm his eyes, against she do appear.	
Puck	I go, I go, look how I go,	
	Swifter than arrow from the Tartar's bow. *He exits.*	
Oberon	Flower of this purple dye,	70
	Hit with Cupid's archery,	
	Sink in apple of his eye.	
	[Squeezing the flower over Demetrius' eyes.]	
	When his love he doth espy,	
	Let her shine as gloriously	
	As the Venus of the sky.	75
	When thou wak'st, if she be by,	
	Beg of her for remedy. *Enter Puck.*	
Puck	Captain of our fairy band,	
	Helena is here at hand,	
	And the youth, mistook by me,	80
	Pleading for a lover's fee.	

40 **cannot be but:** must be
41 **dead:** pale

45 **Venus:** the planet, called 'the evening star'
45 **glimmering sphere:** shining orbit
46 **to:** got to do with

49 **cur:** dog

51 **be never … men:** you don't count as a man
52 **spend … mood:** are angry for no good reason
54 **for aught … tell:** as far as I know
56 **therefore:** for it

59 **no:** not
60 **vein:** mood

65 **look thou:** make sure you
66 **illusion:** trick
67 **against:** ready for when

69 **the tartar's bow:** the Tartars of Central Asia were famous archers

72 **apple:** the pupil

77 **Beg of her for remedy:** plead with her to love you

81 **fee:** payment

A

2 How does Demetrius' description of Helena after he wakes (lines 100–7) show his feelings for her? How is his language different in Act 2 Scene 1 (page 29)?

ABOVE (left to right) Helena, Lysander, Demetrius
One of these photographs was taken at line 100, the other at line 180 (page 57). Which is which? Support your answer with details from what is happening in each place.
BELOW (left to right) Lysander, Helena, Demetrius

B

	Shall we their fond pageant see?
	Lord, what fools these mortals be!
Oberon	Stand aside. The noise they make
	Will cause Demetrius to awake.	85
Puck	Then will two at once woo one,
	That must needs be sport alone.
	And those things do best please me
	That befall prepost'rously.

Enter Lysander and Helena.

Lysander	Why should you think that I should woo in scorn?	90
	Scorn and derision never come in tears.	
	Look when I vow I weep, and vows so born,	
	In their nativity all truth appears.	
Helena	You do advance your cunning more and more.	
	When truth kills truth, O devilish holy fray!	95
	These vows are Hermia's. Will you give her o'er?	
Lysander	I had no judgment when to her I swore.	
Helena	Nor none, in my mind, now you give her o'er.	
Lysander	Demetrius loves her, and he loves not you.	

Demetrius wakes up.

Demetrius	O Helen, goddess, nymph, perfect, divine,	100
	To what, my love, shall I compare thine eyne?	
	Crystal is muddy. O how ripe in show	
	Thy lips, those kissing cherries, tempting grow!	
	That pure congealèd white, high Taurus' snow,	
	Fanned with the eastern wind, turns to a crow	105
	When thou hold'st up thy hand. O, let me kiss	
	This princess of pure white, this seal of bliss.	
Helena	O spite! O hell! I see you all are bent	
	To set against me for your merriment.	
	If you were civil and knew courtesy,	110
	You would not do me thus much injury.	
	If you were men, as men you are in show,	
	You would not use a gentle lady so,	
	To vow, and swear, and superpraise my parts,	
	When I am sure you hate me with your hearts.	115
	You both are rivals, and love Hermia,	
	And now both rivals to mock Helena.	
Lysander	You are unkind, Demetrius. Be not so.	
	For you love Hermia, this you know I know.	
	And here with all good will, with all my heart,	120
	In Hermia's love I yield you up my part.	
	And yours of Helena to me bequeath,	
	Whom I do love, and will do till my death.	

82 **fond pageant:** foolish show

87 **alone:** in itself

89 **befall prepost'rously:** have ridiculous consequences

90 **in scorn:** to mock you
92 **Look:** see how
93 **nativity:** birth
94 **advance:** increase
94 **cunning:** trickery
95 **truth kills truth:** a promise to one person cancels a promise to another
95 **devilish holy fray:** a conflict between true and false promises
96 **o'er:** up

101 **thine eyne:** your eyes

104 **congealèd:** frozen
104 **Taurus:** mountains in Turkey
105 **turns to a crow:** turns black as a crow
107 **princess of pure white:** [her hand]
107 **seal of:** promise of
108 **bent:** decided
109 **To set:** to work together
110 **were civil:** had any manners
113 **use:** treat
114 **parts:** qualities

122 **to me bequeath:** give to me

(Left to right) Lysander, Hermia, Helena at lines 135–9
Who is Lysander talking to, and what is the reaction of each of the women?

3 Rhyme is used in much of this scene, but in the argument between Hermia and Helena (from line 144) rhyme is no longer used. How does this change the atmosphere of the scene?

Helena	Never did mockers waste more idle breath.	
Demetrius	Lysander, keep thy Hermia. I will none.	125
	If e'er I loved her, all that love is gone.	
	My heart to her, but as guest-wise, sojourned,	
	And now to Helen is it home returned,	
	There to remain.	
Lysander	Helena, it is not so.	

Enter Hermia.

Hermia	Thou art not by mine eye, Lysander, found,	130
	Mine ear, I thank it, brought me to thy sound.	
	But why unkindly didst thou leave me so?	
Lysander	Why should he stay, whom love doth press to go?	
Hermia	What love could press Lysander from my side?	
Lysander	Lysander's love (that would not let him bide)	135
	Fair Helena, who more engilds the night	
	Than all you fiery oes and eyes of light.	
	Why seek'st thou me? Could not this make thee know	
	The hate I bear thee made me leave thee so?	
Hermia	You speak not as you think. It cannot be.	140
Helena	Lo, she is one of this confederacy.	
	Now I perceive they have conjoined all three	
	To fashion this false sport in spite of me. —	
	Injurious Hermia, most ungrateful maid,	
	Have you conspired, have you with these contrived	145
	To bait me with this foul derision?	
	Is all the counsel that we two have shared,	
	The sisters' vows, the hours that we have spent,	
	When we have chid the hasty-footed time	
	For parting us. O, is it all forgot?	150
	All school-days' friendship, childhood innocence?	
	And will you rent our ancient love asunder,	
	To join with men in scorning your poor friend?	
	It is not friendly, 'tis not maidenly.	
Hermia	I am amazed at your passionate words.	155
	I scorn you not. It seems that you scorn me.	
Helena	Have you not set Lysander, as in scorn,	
	To follow me and praise my eyes and face?	
	And made your other love, Demetrius,	
	Who even but now did spurn me with his foot,	160
	To call me goddess, nymph, divine and rare,	
	Precious, celestial? Wherefore speaks he this	
	To her he hates? And wherefore doth Lysander	
	Deny your love (so rich within his soul)?	
Hermia	I understand not what you mean by this.	165

125 I will none: I don't want her

127 but as guest-wise, sojourned: was just visiting her for a while

133 press: urge

135 bide: stay
136 more engilds: glows more golden in
137 yon fiery … of light: the stars

141 confederacy: conspiracy
142 conjoined: united
143 fashion: design
143 in spite of: to show their contempt for
144 Injurious: hurtful, unjust
145 contrived: planned
146 bait: persecute
147 counsel: confidences
149 chid: scolded

152 rent: tear
152 asunder: apart

160 even but now: just now
161 rare: exceptional
162 celestial: heavenly
162 Wherefore: why

Lysander and Hermia
Which line might the actor playing Lysander have been speaking when this photograph was taken: line 173, line 182, or line 185? Explain the reasons for your answer.

56

Helena	Ay, do persever. Counterfeit sad looks,	
	Make mouths upon me when I turn my back,	
	Wink each at other, hold the sweet jest up.	
	If you have any pity, grace, or manners,	
	You would not make me such an argument.	170
	But fare ye well. 'Tis partly my own fault,	
	Which death or absence soon shall remedy.	
Lysander	Stay, gentle Helena, hear my excuse,	
	My love, my life, my soul, fair Helena!	
Helena	O excellent!	
Hermia	Sweet, do not scorn her so.	175
Lysander	Helen, I love thee, by my life, I do.	
	I swear by that which I will lose for thee,	
	To prove him false, that says I love thee not.	
Demetrius	I say I love thee more than he can do.	
Lysander	If thou say so, withdraw and prove it too.	180
Demetrius	Quick, come!	
Hermia	Lysander, whereto tends all this?	
	Hermia clings to Lysander.	
Lysander	Hang off thou cat, thou burr. Vile thing let loose,	
	Or I will shake thee from me like a serpent.	
Hermia	Why are you grown so rude? What change is this	
	Sweet love?	
Lysander	Thy love? Out, tawny Tartar, out!	185
	Out loathed medicine! O hated potion hence!	
Hermia	Do you not jest?	
Helena	Yes sooth, and so do you.	
Lysander	Demetrius, I will keep my word with thee.	
Demetrius	I would I had your bond, for I perceive	
	A weak bond holds you. I'll not trust your word.	190
Lysander	What, should I hurt her, strike her, kill her dead?	
	Although I hate her, I'll not harm her so.	
Hermia	What, can you do me greater harm than hate?	
	Hate me? Wherefore? O me, what news, my love?	
	Am not I Hermia? Are not you Lysander?	195
	I am as fair now as I was erewhile.	
	Since night you loved me, yet since night you left me,	
	In earnest, shall I say?	
Lysander	Ay, by my life,	
	And never did desire to see thee more.	
	Therefore be out of hope, of question, of doubt.	200
	Be certain, nothing truer; 'tis no jest	
	That I do hate thee and love Helena.	

166 Ay, do persever: that's it, go on
166 Counterfeit: fake
167 Make mouths upon: pull faces at

170 an argument: a figure of fun

172 remedy: cure

177 by that … lose for thee: by my life

180 withdraw: come away (to fight a duel)

181 whereto tends: what's the point of
182 Hang off: let go
182 burr: rough seed-head that sticks to clothing
182 let loose: let go
184 rude: rough, unkind
185 Tartar: the Tartars of Central Asia were famously fierce
186 loathed medicine: poison
186 potion: mixture
186 hence: go away
187 Do you not jest?: you're joking, aren't you?
187 sooth: truly
189 I would: I wish
189 your bond: your word
190 A weak bond: [Hermia is holding onto him]
191 should I: do you want me to
194 O me: an exclamation of misery
194 what news: what's going on
196 erewhile: before
196 Since night: when night fell
198 In earnest: in all seriousness

200 be out of: have no

ABOVE Helena, as Demetrius and Lysander stop Hermia attacking her, between lines 219–220.
Look back at the photographs of this scene from this production (pages 52, 54 and 56). How have things changed for Helena by this point in the scene?
BELOW Demetrius, Hermia, Lysander, Helena, lines 231–2

58

Hermia	O me! *[To Helena.]* You juggler, you canker-blossom,
	You thief of love! What, have you come by night
	And stolen my love's heart from him?
Helena	Fine, i' faith. 205
	Have you no modesty, no maiden shame,
	No touch of bashfulness? What, will you tear
	Impatient answers from my gentle tongue?
	Fie, fie, you counterfeit. You puppet, you!
Hermia	"Puppet"? Why so? Ay, that way goes the game. 210
	Now I perceive that she hath made compare
	Between our statures. She hath urged her height,
	And with her personage, her tall personage,
	Her height, forsooth, she hath prevailed with him.
	And are you grown so high in his esteem 215
	Because I am so dwarfish and so low?
	How low am I, thou painted maypole? Speak!
	How low am I? I am not yet so low
	But that my nails can reach unto thine eyes.

She runs at Helena.

Helena	I pray you, though you mock me, gentlemen, 220
	Let her not hurt me. You perhaps may think,
	Because she is something lower than myself,
	That I can match her.
Hermia	Lower? Hark again.
Helena	Good Hermia, do not be so bitter with me.
Lysander	Be not afraid, she shall not harm thee Helena. 225
Demetrius	No, sir, she shall not, though you take her part.
Helena	O, when she is angry, she is keen and shrewd.
	And though she be but little, she is fierce.
Hermia	"Little" again? Nothing but "low" and "little"?
	Why will you suffer her to flout me thus? 230
	Let me come to her!
Lysander	Get you gone: you dwarf,
	You minimus of hind'ring knot-grass made,
	You bead, you acorn.
Demetrius	You are too officious
	In her behalf that scorns your services.
	Let her alone. Speak not of Helena, 235
	Take not her part. For if thou dost intend
	Never so little show of love to her,
	Thou shalt a-buy it.
Lysander	Now she holds me not.
	Now follow, if thou dar'st, to try whose right,
	Of thine or mine, is most in Helena. 240

203 **juggler:** trickster
203 **canker-blossom:** flower-eating grub
205 **Fine, i'faith:** oh, well done

209 **Fie, fie:** For shame
209 **counterfeit:** false friend
210 **Why so?:** so that's it?
212 **statures:** heights
213 **personage:** size, appearance
214 **prevailed with him:** won him over
215 **esteem:** opinion
216 **low:** short
216 **painted maypole:** tall, skinny person, covered in make-up

223 **match her:** equal her in a fight

226 **part:** side
227 **keen:** bitter or sharp
227 **shrewd:** quarrelsome
228 **though:** even though

230 **suffer:** allow
230 **flout:** insult
232 **minimus:** speck
232 **hind'ring knot-grass:** creeping, clinging grass
233–4 **officious In her behalf:** pushy about helping

237 **never so little:** even the slightest
238 **a-buy it:** pay dearly for it
239–40 **to try whose right … in Helena:** to fight for the right to court Helena

ABOVE Helena runs away from Hermia, lines 245–6.

Within the two lines given for each photo, pick a line or a half-line to use as an alternative caption.

BELOW Oberon punishes Puck, lines 248–9.

Demetrius	Follow? Nay, I'll go with thee cheek by jowl.

Exit Lysander and Demetrius.

Hermia	You, mistress, all this coil is long of you.
	Nay, go not back.
Helena	I will not trust you, I,
	Nor longer stay in your curst company.
	Your hands than mine are quicker for a fray, 245
	My legs are longer though, to run away. *She runs off.*
Hermia	I am amazed, and know not what to say. *She exits.*

Oberon and Puck move forward.

Oberon	This is thy negligence. Still thou mistak'st,
	Or else committ'st thy knaveries wilfully.
Puck	Believe me, king of shadows, I mistook. 250
	Did not you tell me I should know the man
	By the Athenian garments he had on?
	And so far blameless proves my enterprise,
	That I have 'nointed an Athenian's eyes.
Oberon	Thou see'st these lovers seek a place to fight. 255
	Hie therefore, Robin, overcast the night,
	The starry welkin cover thou anon
	With drooping fog as black as Acheron,
	And lead these testy rivals so astray
	As one come not within another's way. 260
	Till o'er their brows death-counterfeiting sleep
	With leaden legs and batty wings doth creep.
	Then crush this herb into Lysander's eye,
	Whose liquor hath this virtuous property,
	To take from thence all error with his might, 265
	And make his eyeballs roll with wonted sight.
	When they next wake, all this derision
	Shall seem a dream and fruitless vision.
	Whiles I in this affair do thee employ,
	I'll to my Queen, and beg her Indian boy. 270
	And then I will her charmèd eye release
	From monster's view, and all things shall be peace.

He exits.

Puck	Up and down, up and down,
	I will lead them up and down.
	I am fear'd in field and town. 275
	Goblin, lead them up and down.
	Here comes one.

Enter Lysander.

Lysander	Where art thou, proud Demetrius? Speak thou now.

241 cheek by jowl: side-by-side

242 coil: trouble
242 long of you: your fault

245 a fray: a fight

249 committ'st … wilfully: you're doing this deliberately

253 my enterprise: my actions
256 Hie: hurry
257 welkin: sky
258 drooping: falling
258 Acheron: a river in the Underworld (Hell in Greek myths)
259 testy: bad-tempered
260 As one come … another's way: so they never meet
262 batty: bat-like
264 virtuous property: beneficial effect
265 his: its
266 his eyeballs … sight: him look, and feel, as he used to
267 derision: scornful squabbling

276 Goblin: [he means himself]

Demetrius and Puck, lines 295–9
How do you know who is in control?

4 What effect do the short speeches and the use of half lines have on the way the scene progresses?

Puck	*[Imitating Demetrius' voice.]* Here villain, drawn and ready. Where art thou?
Lysander	I will be with thee straight.
Puck	Follow me, then, 280 To plainer ground. *Lysander exits, following the voice.* *Enter Demetrius.*
Demetrius	Lysander, speak again! Thou runaway, thou coward, art thou fled? Speak! In some bush? Where dost thou hide thy head?
Puck	*[Imitating Lysander's voice.]* Thou coward, art thou bragging to the stars? Telling the bushes that thou look'st for wars, 285 And wilt not come? Come recreant, come, thou child, I'll whip thee with a rod.
Demetrius	Yea, art thou there?
Puck	Follow my voice, we'll try no manhood here. *They exit.* *Enter Lysander.*
Lysander	The villain is much lighter-heeled than I, I followed fast, but faster he did fly, 290 That fallen am I in dark uneven way, And here will rest me. *[He lies down.]* Come, thou gentle day, For if but once thou show me thy grey light, I'll find Demetrius and revenge this spite. *[He sleeps].* *Enter Puck and Demetrius.*
Puck	*[Imitating Lysander's voice.]* Ho, ho, ho! Coward, why com'st thou not? 295
Demetrius	Abide me, if thou dar'st. For well I wot Thou runn'st before me, shifting every place, And dar'st not stand, nor look me in the face. Where art thou now?
Puck	Come hither, I am here. 299
Demetrius	Nay, then, thou mock'st me. Thou shalt buy this dear, If ever I thy face by daylight see. Now, go thy way. Faintness constraineth me To measure out my length on this cold bed. *[Lies down].* By day's approach look to be visited. *[He sleeps.]* *Enter Helena.*
Helena	O weary night, O long and tedious night, 305 Abate thy hours! Shine comforts from the east, That I may back to Athens by daylight, From these that my poor company detest. And sleep, that sometimes shuts up sorrow's eye,

---

279 drawn: with my sword drawn

280 straight: straight away
281 plainer: flatter, more open

285 look'st for wars: want to fight
286 recreant: coward

287 whip … a rod: beat you like a schoolboy
288 we'll try no manhood here: this isn't the right place to fight
289 lighter-heeled: quicker on his feet

291 That: and now

294 revenge this spite: punish him for leading me here

296 Abide me: wait for me
296 well I wot: I know quite well
297 before: in front of

300 buy this dear: pay for this
302 go thy way: do what you like
302 constraineth: forces
303 measure out my length: lie down
304 look to be visited: expect to be found

306 Abate: shorten
306 Shine … the east: send comforting daylight

Puck and Hermia, lines 316–20
Compare this photograph with the last one showing Hermia in this production (page 50). How does her costume help the audience understand what has happened to her?

These questions are about all of Act 3 Scene 2.

5 How would you advise the actors playing Helena and Hermia to show the change in the relationship through how they say their lines and move on the stage?

6 In Shakespeare's time, many people believed that woods were filled with magic creatures. How might the affect the reaction of an audience at the time to the way Puck's actions make so many problems for the human characters?

7 What do the events of this scene add to the themes of magic and the difficulties facing lovers?

8 How does Oberon's behaviour in this scene develop our understanding of his character?

	Steal me awhile from mine own company.	**310**

She lies down and sleeps.

Puck Yet but three? Come one more,
Two of both kinds make up four.
Here she comes, curst and sad.
Cupid is a knavish lad,
Thus to make poor females mad. **315**

Enter Hermia.

Hermia Never so weary, never so in woe,
Bedabbled with the dew and torn with briers,
I can no further crawl, no further go.
My legs can keep no pace with my desires. **319**
Here will I rest me, till the break of day.*[Lying down.]*
Heavens shield Lysander, if they mean a fray.

She sleeps.

Puck On the ground
Sleep sound.
I'll apply
To your eye, **325**
Gentle lover, remedy.

[Squeezing the juice on Lysander's eyes.]

When thou wak'st,
Thou tak'st
True delight
In the sight **330**
Of thy former lady's eye.
And the country proverb known,
That every man should take his own,
In your waking shall be shown.
Jack shall have Jill, **335**
Nought shall go ill,
The man shall have his mare again, and all shall be well.

Exit Puck, leaving the lovers sleeping
on the stage.

313 curst: cross

317 Bedabbled: splattered
317 briers: brambles
319 can keep …my desires: can't keep going
321 a fray: to fight

334 shall be shown: will be proved right
336 nought shall go ill: nothing will go wrong
337 the man … mare again: proverb for things turning out all right

---

These questions ask you to reflect on all of Act 3.

a) How are words and imagery used to create the different feelings of magic, confusion and dispute in Act 3?

b) Who do you feel sympathetic towards in Act 3? Explain the reasons for your answer.

c) Think about how magic is used in this Act. Is it being used for the right or the wrong reasons? Explain the reasons for your answer.

d) How is the atmosphere of confusion and conflict created in Act 3?

e) What does an audience learn about the relationship between Puck and Oberon during Act 3?

Titania, Peaseblossom, and Bottom, lines 1–4
How many of Shakespeare's stage directions in text has the
director followed? (See page 48 to check what they are.)

Act 4 Scene 1

Lysander, Demetrius, Helena, and Hermia are still sleeping.

Enter Titania, Bottom, Peaseblossom, Cobweb, Moth Mustardseed, and other Fairies, and Oberon, unseen, behind them.

Titania	Come, sit thee down upon this flowery bed,	
	While I thy amiable cheeks do coy,	
	And stick musk-roses in thy sleek smooth head,	
	And kiss thy fair large ears, my gentle joy.	
	What, wilt thou hear some music, my sweet love?	5
Bottom	I have a reasonable good ear in music. Let's have the tongs and the bones.	

Simple rural music starts.

Titania	Or say, sweet love, what thou desir'st to eat.	
Bottom	Truly, a peck of provender. I could munch your good dry oats.	10
Titania	I have a venturous fairy, that shall seek	
	The squirrel's hoard,	
Bottom	I had rather have a handful of dried peas. But, I pray you, let none of your people stir me, I have an exposition of sleep come upon me.	15
Titania	Sleep thou, and I will wind thee in my arms.	
	Fairies, begone, and be all ways away. *The Fairies exit.*	
	O, how I love thee! How I dote on thee!	

Titania and Bottom sleep, on a different part of the stage to the lovers.

Enter Puck, going to Oberon.

Oberon	Welcome, good Robin. See'st thou this sweet sight?	
	Her dotage now I do begin to pity.	20
	For meeting her of late behind the wood,	
	Seeking sweet favours for this hateful fool,	
	I did upbraid her and fall out with her.	
	When I had at my pleasure taunted her,	
	And she in mild terms begged my patience,	25
	I then did ask of her her changeling child,	
	Which straight she gave me, and her fairy sent	
	To bear him to my bower in Fairy Land.	
	And now I have the boy, I will undo	
	This hateful imperfection of her eyes.	30
	And, gentle Puck, take this transformèd scalp,	
	From off the head of this Athenian swain,	
	That he, awaking when the other do,	
	May all to Athens back again repair,	

What's just happened

- Titania (who is drugged) is madly in love with Bottom. She has given the Indian Boy to Oberon.
- The four lovers are asleep in the woods.
- Theseus is planning an early morning hunt in the woods.

How much do Puck and Oberon know?

2 **amiable:** loveable
2 **coy:** stroke
7 **tongs:** metal musical instrument, like a modern triangle
7 **bones:** pieces of bone played like modern castanets
9 **a peck of provender:** a portion of animal food
11 **venturous:** daring

14 **stir:** disturb
14 **exposition of:** he means 'disposition to' (desire to)

17 **and be all ways away:** scatter in all directions

20 **dotage:** wild infatuation

22 **favours:** presents

31 **transformèd scalp:** [the ass's head]
32 **swain:** man
33 **other:** others
34 **repair:** return

Oberon gives Titania the antidote, while Bottom sleeps and Puck watches.

Compare giving the drugs in this production with the two photographs of giving the drugs in the 2008 production (pages 32 and 34). What is the difference? Why do you think the director made that choice?

	And think no more of this night's accidents	35
	But as the fierce vexation of a dream.	
	But first I will release the Fairy Queen.	
	[Squeezing the flower on Titania's eyes.]	
	Be as thou wast wont to be,	
	See as thou wast wont to see.	
	Dian's bud, or Cupid's flower	40
	Hath such force and blessed power.	
	Now my Titania, wake you, my sweet queen.	
Titania	My Oberon, what visions have I seen!	
	Methought I was enamoured of an ass.	
Oberon	There lies your love.	
Titania	How came these things to pass?	45
	O, how mine eyes do loathe his visage now!	
Oberon	Silence awhile. Robin, take off this head.	
	Titania, music call, and strike more dead	
	Than common sleep of all these five the sense.	
Titania	Music, ho! Music such as charmeth sleep.	50
	The rural music stops.	
Puck	*[Taking off the ass-head.]*	
	Now, when thou wak'st, with thine own fool's eyes peep.	
Oberon	*[Different music starts, Oberon and Titania dance.]*	
	Now, thou and I are new in amity,	
	And will tomorrow midnight, solemnly	
	Dance in Duke Theseus' house triumphantly,	
	And bless it to all fair prosperity.	55
	There shall the pairs of faithful lovers be	
	Wedded, with Theseus, all in jollity.	
	Oberon, Titania, and Puck exit.	
	The lovers and Bottom continue to sleep.	
	Hunting horns sound offstage.	
	Enter Theseus, Hippolyta, Egeus, and followers.	
Theseus	We will, fair queen, up to the mountain's top,	
	And mark the musical confusion	
	Of hounds and echo in conjunction.	60
	[He sees the lovers.]	
	But, soft, what nymphs are these?	
Egeus	My lord, this is my daughter here asleep,	
	And this Lysander, this Demetrius is,	
	This Helena, old Nedar's Helena.	
	I wonder of their being here together.	65
Theseus	No doubt they rose up early to observe	
	The rite of May, and hearing our intent,	

36 fierce vexation: upsetting memory

38 thou wast wont: you used

40 Dian's bud: the antidote
40 Cupid's flower: the original drug

44 enamoured of: in love with

45 pass: happen
46 visage: face

48–9 strike more dead … the sense: make Bottom and the lovers sleep very deeply

52 new in amity: friends again

55 to all fair prosperity: so they do well

58 We will: we'll go

60 in conjunction: at the same time

61 soft: wait a minute
61 nymphs: woodland spirits

65 of: at

ABOVE (left to right) Demetrius, Helena, Hermia, Lysander
One photograph was taken between lines 72–4, and the other about line 108. Which is which? Explain the reasons for your answer.
BELOW (left to right) Helena, Demetrius, Egeus, Hippolyta, Theseus, Hermia (hidden by) Lysander.

Betrothal

Betrothal was when a man and woman promised, in front of witnesses, to marry each other. It was much more serious than a modern engagement. Not all couples were betrothed, but many were, especially those from wealthy and important families. People saw breaking a betrothal (which Demetrius admits to in line 105) as very wrong.

	Came here in grace of our solemnity.	
	But speak Egeus, is not this the day	
	That Hermia should give answer of her choice?	70
Egeus	It is, my lord.	
Theseus	Go, bid the huntsmen wake them with their horns.	
	A servant exits. Horns offstage, Lysander, Demetrius, Helena, and Hermia wake up; then a shout offstage makes them start.	
	Good morrow friends. Saint Valentine is past,	
	Begin these wood-birds but to couple now?	
Lysander	Pardon, my lord. *[The lovers kneel to Theseus.]*	
Theseus	I pray you all, stand up.	75
	I know you two are rival enemies.	
	How comes this gentle concord in the world,	
	That hatred is so far from jealousy,	
	To sleep by hate, and fear no enmity?	
Lysander	My lord, I shall reply amazedly,	80
	Half sleep, half waking. But as yet, I swear,	
	I cannot truly say how I came here.	
	But as I think, (for truly would I speak)	
	I came with Hermia hither. Our intent	
	Was to be gone from Athens, where we might	85
	Without the peril of the Athenian law —	
Egeus	Enough, enough, my lord. You have enough.	
	I beg the law, the law, upon his head.	
	They would have stol'n away. — They would, Demetrius,	
	Thereby to have defeated you and me.	90
	You of your wife, and me of my consent,	
	Of my consent, that she should be your wife.	
Demetrius	My lord, fair Helen told me of their stealth,	
	Of this their purpose hither to this wood,	
	And I in fury hither followed them,	95
	Fair Helena in fancy following me.	
	But my good lord, I wot not by what power,	
	But by some power it is, my love to Hermia,	
	Melted as the snow, seems to me now	
	As the remembrance of an idle gaud	100
	Which in my childhood I did dote upon.	
	And all the faith, the virtue of my heart,	
	The object and the pleasure of mine eye,	
	Is only Helena. To her, my lord,	
	Was I betrothed ere I saw Hermia.	105
Theseus	Fair lovers, you are fortunately met.	
	Of this discourse we more will hear anon.	
	Egeus, I will overbear your will,	

68 in grace of our solemnity: to attend our celebrations

73 Saint Valentine: Saint Valentine's Day (14 February) traditionally said to be when birds choose mates

74 couple: pair off

77 gentle concord: friendliness
78 jealousy: suspicion
79 by hate … no enmity: beside the person who hates him with no fear of harm

83 truly would I speak: I want to tell the exact truth
84 hither: here

90 Thereby: by doing so
90 defeated: cheated

93 stealth: secretly running away

96 in fancy: because of love
97 I wot not: I don't know

100 remembrance: memory
100 idle gaud: cheap toy

107 discourse: story
107 anon: later
108 overbear your will: overrule you

Bottom, soon after he wakes up.
Pick a phrase from Bottom's speech
(lines 125–36) which would be a good
caption.

These questions are about all of Act 4 Scene 1.

1. How do the words and images used by the four lovers and by Bottom at the end of the scene show that they all feel they have experienced a dream?

2. Look at lines 125–136. How would you tell the actor playing Bottom to speak and move to create the sense of awaking from a strange dream?

3. In Shakespeare's time, fathers usually chose husbands for their daughters. How might an audience at the time feel about Theseus overruling Egeus (think back to the first scene)?

4. How is the theme of the difficulties of true love brought to a conclusion in this scene?

5. Why does Oberon decide to release Titania from the spell and how does this affect the audience's view of him?

What's just happened

- The rehearsal in the wood broke up in terror and confusion.
- Quince and the actors fled back to Athens.
- The next day is the day they hope to perform their play at Theseus' wedding.

How will the actors feel?

	109 by and by: soon
For in the temple, by and by with us	**110 eternally be knit:** be married
These couples shall eternally be knit. **110**	
Come Hippolyta.	

Theseus, Hippolyta, Egeus, and followers exit.

Demetrius These things seem small and undistinguishable,
Like far off mountains turnèd into clouds.

Hermia Methinks I see these things with parted eye,
When every thing seems double.

114 with parted eye: out of focus

Helena   So methinks. **115**
And I have found Demetrius like a jewel,
Mine own, and not mine own.

Demetrius   Are you sure
That we are awake? It seems to me
That yet we sleep, we dream. Do not you think
The Duke was here, and bid us follow him? **120**

119 yet we sleep: we're still sleeping

Hermia Yea, and my father.

Helena   And Hippolyta.

Lysander And he did bid us follow to the temple.

Demetrius Why then we are awake. Let's follow him,
And by the way let us recount our dreams.

The Lovers exit. Bottom wakes up.

124 by the way: on the way
124 recount: tell each other
128 God's my life!: God save my life (a mild oath)
128 hence: away from here
129 rare vision: amazing, vivid dream
129–30 past the wit … it was: beyond understanding
132 a patched fool: a king's jester (they wore patchwork clothes)
133 offer: try
134 ballad: song
135 it hath no bottom: you can't get to the bottom of it
136 in the latter end: towards the end of

Bottom When my cue comes, call me, and I will answer. My next **125** is, "Most fair Pyramus." Heigh-ho! Peter Quince? Flute, the bellows-mender? Snout, the tinker? Starveling? God's my life! Stolen hence, and left me asleep. I have had a most rare vision. I have had a dream, past the wit of man to say what dream it was. Methought I was — **130** there is no man can tell what. Methought I was, — and methought I had… (but man is but a patched fool, if he will offer to say what methought I had). I will get Peter Quince to write a ballad of this dream. It shall be called Bottom's Dream, because it hath no bottom. And I will **135** sing it in the latter end of a play, before the Duke.

He exits.

Act 4 Scene 2

Enter Quince, Flute, Snout, and Starveling.

Quince Have you sent to Bottom's house? Is he come home yet?

Starveling He cannot be heard of. Out of doubt he is transported.

Flute If he come not, then the play is marred. It goes not forward, doth it?

Quince It is not possible. You have not a man in all Athens able to discharge Pyramus but he. **6**

Enter Bottom.

2 He cannot be heard of: no one knows where he is
2 Out of doubt: certainly
2 transported: carried off or transformed
3 marred: spoiled
3–4 It goes not forward, doth it?: we can't put it on, can we?
6 discharge: play the part of

73

Left to right: Bottom, Quince, Snug, Flute, and Snout (Starveling is behind Quince). Which phrase is Bottom most likely to be speaking when this photograph was taken?

- *Where are these lads?*
- *Not a word of me.*
- *Away! Go, away!*

Bottom	Where are these lads? Where are these hearts? Masters, I am to discourse wonders, but ask me not what. For if I tell you, I am no true Athenian. I will tell you everything, right as it fell out. **10**
Quince	Let us hear, sweet Bottom.
Bottom	Not a word of me. All that I will tell you is, that the Duke hath dined. Get your apparel together, good strings to your beards, new ribbons to your pumps, meet presently at the palace, every man look o'er his **15** part. For the short and the long is, our play is preferred! In any case let Thisbe have clean linen, and let not him that plays the lion pare his nails, for they shall hang out for the lion's claws. And most dear actors, eat no onions nor garlic, for we are to utter sweet breath, and I do not doubt but to hear them say, it is a sweet comedy. No **21** more words. Away! Go, away!

Exit all.

7 **hearts:** good friends
8 **discourse:** tell you

10 **right as it fell out:** just as it happened
12 **of:** out of
13 **apparel:** costumes
14 **strings:** to tie on false beards
14 **ribbons:** laces
14 **pumps:** light, indoor shoes
15 **presently:** straight away
15 **look o'er:** make sure he knows
16 **preferred:** recommended
18 **pare:** cut

These questions are about all of Act 4 Scene 2.

1 Read lines 125–136. How does Bottom's speech show the audience his state of mind?

2 How would you tell the actors playing Quince and the other workmen to speak and move when Bottom suddenly arrives?

3 When the play was written, wealthy and important people often asked groups of actors to put on plays for them. How would an audience at that time feel about the play by Bottom and the other workmen being chosen by the Duke instead of a more experienced group of actors?

4 How is the sense of things being turned upside down brought to an end when Bottom goes back to organising their performance?

5 Bottom does not talk to the others about his amazing experiences, but instead gets on with planning the play for Theseus. What does this show the audience about his character?

These questions ask you to reflect on all of Act 4.

a) How is the metaphor of eyes and seeing things differently developed in Act 4?

b) How is love represented in Act 4?

c) Demetrius says to the other lovers *'let us recount our dreams'*. How do they explain what has happened to them?

d) How does Oberon and Titania's relationship change during Act 4?

e) Most of the dialogue is delivered by male characters in Act 4. Why do you think Shakespeare did this; how does it reflect the world of the play?

Hippolyta and Theseus enter after their wedding.
How has the director taken inspiration from modern royal weddings?

Act 5 Scene 1

Enter Theseus, Hippolyta, with Philostrate and other lords and attendants.

Hippolyta	'Tis strange, my Theseus, that these lovers speak of.
Theseus	More strange than true. I never may believe
	These antic fables, nor these fairy toys.
	Lovers and madmen have such seething brains,
	Such shaping fantasies, that apprehend **5**
	More than cool reason ever comprehends.
	The lunatic, the lover and the poet
	Are of imagination all compact.
Hippolyta	But all the story of the night told over,
	And all their minds transfigured so together, **10**
	More witnesseth than fancy's images
	And grows to something of great constancy.

Enter Lysander, Demetrius, Hermia and Helena.

Theseus	Here come the lovers, full of joy and mirth. —
	Joy, gentle friends, joy and fresh days of love
	Accompany your hearts.
Lysander	More than to us **15**
	Wait in your royal walks, your board, your bed.
Theseus	Come now, what masques, what dances shall we have,
	To wear away this long age of three hours
	Between our after-supper and bedtime?
	Call Philostrate.
Philostrate	Here, mighty Theseus. **20**
Theseus	What masque? What music? How shall we beguile
	The lazy time if not with some delight?
Philostrate	*[Handing Theseus a piece of paper.]*
	There is a brief how many sports are ripe.
	Make choice of which your Highness will see first.
Theseus	*[Reading.] The battle with the Centaurs, to be sung* **25**
	By an Athenian eunuch to the harp.
	We'll none of that.
	[Reading.] The riot of the tipsy Bacchanals,
	Tearing the Thracian singer in their rage.
	That is an old device, and it was played **30**
	When I from Thebes came last a conqueror.
	[Reading.] A tedious brief scene of young Pyramus
	And his love Thisbe. Very tragical mirth.
	Merry and tragical? Tedious and brief?
	That is, hot ice and wondrous strange snow. **35**
	How shall we find the concord of this discord?

What's just happened

- Theseus, Hippolyta and the lovers have returned to Athens from the wood.
- The three couples have been married.
- Quince and his actors have gone to the court having heard their play has been chosen.

1   **that:** the things

3   **antic fables:** bizarre stories

3   **airy toys:** childish stories about fairies

4   **seething:** churning

5   **shaping fantasies:** inventive imaginations

5   **apprehend:** seem to understand

8   **Are of … all compact:** are made up entirely by imagination

10   **transfigured:** changed

10   **together:** in the same way

11   **More witnesseth:** is evidence of more

11   **fancy's images:** imagined events

12   **constancy:** reliability

16   **board:** dining table

17   **masques:** entertainments with dancing and music

23   **brief:** summary

23   **sports:** entertainments

23   **ripe:** ready for performance

35   **That is:** that's like saying

36   **concord:** agreement

36   **discord:** disagreement

Court performance

Shakespeare's company made a profit by performing plays for the public, in a theatre. Sometimes, though, they were called to perform for the monarch and the courtiers at the royal court. They also performed in the homes of wealthy and important people when they went on tour. They were well paid for these shows. However, the audience may well have been as disruptive as they are here.

Quince leads on the actors, Snug to the left and Starveling leaning out on the right, 2012 production.

Quince and his cast are usually called the Mechanicals, because they all had trades in Athens. What impression do you think their costumes would have on Theseus, Hippolyta, and the other courtiers?

Philostrate	A play there is, my lord, some ten words long,
	Which is as brief as I have known a play,
	But by ten words, my lord, it is too long,
	Which makes it tedious, for in all the play **40**
	There is not one word apt, one player fitted.
	And tragical, my noble lord, it is,
	For Pyramus therein doth kill himself.
	Which when I saw rehearsed, I must confess,
	Made mine eyes water, but more merry tears **45**
	The passion of loud laughter never shed.
Theseus	What are they that do play it?
Philostrate	Hard-handed men that work in Athens here,
	Which never laboured in their minds till now.
Theseus	And we will hear it.
Philostrate	No, my noble lord, **50**
	It is not for you. I have heard it over,
	And it is nothing, nothing in the world.
Theseus	I will hear that play.
	For never anything can be amiss,
	When simpleness and duty tender it. **55**
	Go bring them in — and take your places, ladies.

Exit Philostrate.

Hippolyta	I love not to see wretchedness o'ercharged,
	And duty in his service perishing.
Theseus	Why gentle sweet, you shall see no such thing.
Hippolyta	He says they can do nothing in this kind. **60**
Theseus	The kinder we, to give them thanks for nothing.

Enter Philostrate.

Philostrate	So please your grace, the Prologue is addressed.
Theseus	Let him approach.

Trumpets sound offstage.

Enter Quince as the Prologue.

Prologue	*[He speaks badly, ignoring the punctuation.]*
(Quince)	*If we offend, it is with our good will.*
	That you should think, we come not to offend, **65**
	But with good will. To show our simple skill,
	That is the true beginning of our end.
	Consider then, we come but in despite.
	We do not come, as minding to content you,
	Our true intent is. All for your delight, **70**
	We are not here. That you should here repent you,
	The actors are at hand, and, by their show,
	You shall know all, that you are like to know.

41 **fitted:** suitable for his part

54 **never … be amiss:** nothing can ever be wrong
55 **simpleness:** innocence
55 **tender:** offer
57 **wretchedness o'ercharged:** humble people stretched beyond their limit
58 **perishing:** failing
60 **He:** [Philostrate]
60 **in this kind:** of this sort

62 **addressed:** ready

64–5 **good will. That:** a misplaced full stop mangles the sense. This happens several times in the play of Pyramus and Thisbe
67 **our end:** our aim
68 **in despite:** maliciously
69 **as minding:** intending
71 **repent you:** regret your choice

'In this same interlude, it doth befall, That I, one Snout (by name) present a wall.' (lines 105–6).

ABOVE 2008 production

BELOW 2012 production

In what ways have these productions followed the stage directions in text (including lines 82–3)?

What impression of each version of the Mechanicals' play do these photographs give you?

Who is Shakespeare making fun of?

In this scene, Shakespeare is clearly making fun of amateur actors – their fears and their overacting. He could also be making fun of aristocratic audiences. When performing at the royal court, or the homes of the wealthy when on tour, Shakespeare and his company may have suffered from audiences who were more concerned about the effect they were having on each other than attending to the play.

1 How do the comments used by Theseus, Hippolyta and Demetrius on page 81 show their feelings about the play they are watching?

2 Explain how you feel Shakespeare presents them — sympathetically or not?

Theseus	This fellow doth not stand upon points.
Hippolyta	Indeed he hath played on his prologue like a child on a 75 recorder, a sound, but not in government.
Theseus	Who is next?

Enter a trumpeter, followed by Bottom as
Pyramus, Flute as Thisbe, Snout as Wall,
Starveling as Moonshine, and Snug as the Lion.

Prologue (Quince)	*Gentles, perchance you wonder at this show,*
	But wonder on, till truth make all things plain.
	This man is Pyramus, if you would know. 80
	This beauteous lady, Thisbe is certain.
	This man, with lime and rough-cast, doth present
	Wall, that vile wall which did these lovers sunder.
	And through Wall's chink (poor souls) they are content
	To whisper. At the which, let no man wonder. 85
	This man, with lantern, dog, and bush of thorn,
	Presenteth Moonshine. For if you will know,
	By moonshine did these lovers think no scorn
	To meet at Ninus' tomb, there, there to woo.
	This grisly beast (which Lion hight by name) 90
	The trusty Thisbe, coming first by night,
	Did scare away, or rather did affright.
	And as she fled, her mantle she did fall;
	Which Lion vile with bloody mouth did stain.
	Anon comes Pyramus, sweet youth and tall, 95
	And finds his trusty Thisbe's mantle slain;
	Whereat, with blade, with bloody blameful blade,
	He bravely broached his boiling bloody breast,
	And Thisbe, tarrying in mulberry shade,
	His dagger drew, and died. For all the rest, 100
	Let Lion, Moonshine, Wall, and lovers twain,
	At large discourse, while here they do remain.

Exit Quince as Prologue, Bottom as Pyramus,
Flute as Thisbe, Starveling as Moonshine,
and Snug as the Lion.

Theseus	I wonder if the lion be to speak.
Demetrius	No wonder, my lord. One lion may, when many asses do.
Wall (Snout)	*In this same interlude, it doth befall,* 105
	That I, one Snout (by name) present a wall.
	And such a wall, as I would have you think,
	That had in it a crannied hole or chink,
	Through which the lovers, Pyramus and Thisbe
	Did whisper often, very secretly. 110
	And this the cranny is, right and sinister,
	Through which the fearful lovers are to whisper.

74 **stand upon points:** bother about details [here referring to punctuation]

76 **not in government:** out of control

78 *Gentles:* ladies and gentlemen

78 *perchance:* maybe

83 *sunder:* divide, keep apart

87 *Presenteth:* represents

87 *if you will know:* you need to know

88 *think no scorn:* see as no disgrace

90 *grisly:* terrifying

90 *hight:* is called

93 *mantle:* cloak

93 *she did fall:* she dropped

95 *Anon:* instantly

95 *tall:* brave

97 *Whereat:* on seeing this

98 *broached:* stabbed

99 *tarrying:* waiting

99 *mulberry shade:* the shadow of a mulberry tree

101 *lovers twain:* the two lovers

102 *At large discourse:* tell the story at length

104 **No wonder:** It wouldn't surprise me

105 *interlude:* short play

108 *crannied hole:* the first of many puns on 'hole' and the idea of a vagina or anus

111 *sinister:* left

A

ABOVE line 138, 2008 production
In both productions, because of his costume, Wall was unable to put his hand forward to make the chink for Pyramus and Thisbe to talk through. Read lines 130–140. IWhat evidence, if any, shows that Shakespeare intended this section to be played like this?
BELOW line 139, 2012 production

B

Enter Bottom as Pyramus.

Pyramus (Bottom)	*O grim-looked night, O night with hue so black,*
	O night, which ever art, when day is not.
	O night, O night, alack, alack, alack, **115**
	I fear my Thisbe's promise is forgot.
	And thou, O wall, O sweet, O lovely wall,
	That stand'st between her father's ground and mine.
	Thou wall, O wall, O sweet and lovely wall, **119**
	Show me thy chink, to blink through with mine eyne.
	Thanks, courteous wall. Jove shield thee well for this.
	[Kneeling, facing Wall.]
	But what see I? No Thisbe do I see.
	O wicked wall, through whom I see no bliss,
	Cursed be thy stones for thus deceiving me.
Theseus	The wall methinks being sensible, should curse again. **125**
Bottom	No, in truth sir, he should not. Deceiving me is Thisbe's cue. She is to enter now, and I am to spy her through the wall. You shall see, it will fall pat as I told you.
	Enter Flute as Thisbe.
	Yonder she comes.
Thisbe (Flute)	*O wall, full often hast thou heard my moans,* **130**
	For parting my fair Pyramus, and me.
	My cherry lips have often kissed thy stones,
	Thy stones with lime and hair knit up in thee.
Pyramus (Bottom)	*I see a voice. Now will I to the chink,*
	To spy and I can hear my Thisbe's face. **135**
	Thisbe?
Thisbe (Flute)	*My love? Thou art my love I think.*
Pyramus (Bottom)	*Think what thou wilt, I am thy lover's grace.*
	O kiss me through the hole of this vile wall.
Thisbe (Flute)	*[Kneeling to kiss him through the Wall.]*
	I kiss the wall's hole, not your lips at all.
Pyramus (Bottom)	*Wilt thou at Ninny's tomb meet me straightway?* **140**
Thisbe (Flute)	*'Tide life, 'tide death, I come without delay.*
	Exit Pyramus (Bottom) and Thisbe (Flute) in different directions.
Wall (Snout)	*Thus have I, Wall, my part dischargèd so,*
	And being done, thus Wall away doth go.
	Exit Snout as Wall.
Hippolyta	This is the silliest stuff that ever I heard.
Theseus	The best in this kind are but shadows, and the worst are no worse, if imagination amend them. **146**

113 hue: colour
114 art: is
115 alack: an expression of misery

118 ground: land

121 Jove: king of the gods in Roman myths

124 stones: pun on 'stones', another word for 'testicles'
125 sensible: able to have feelings
125 again: in return

128 fall pat: work out exactly

129 Yonder: there

135 and: if

141 'Tide: come

144 in this kind: of this sort
145 shadows: double meaning:
  1) reflections of reality; 2) actors
146 amend: improve

A

B

Snug as the Lion
LEFT 2008 production,
RIGHT 2012 production
Both these photographs were taken as the actor said:
'Then know that I, one Snug the joiner am'.
In the 2012 production, Snug was played by a woman, in 2008 (and in Shakespeare's day) he was played by a man. What difference does it make when we change the sex of a character in a production?

Hippolyta	It must be your imagination then, and not theirs.
	Enter Snug as Lion and Starveling as Moonshine.
Theseus	Here come two noble beasts in, a man and a lion.
Lion (Snug)	*You, ladies, you (whose gentle hearts do fear)*
	When lion rough in wildest rage doth roar. 150
	Then know that I, one Snug the joiner am
	A lion fell.
	For, if I should as lion come in strife
	Into this place, 'twere pity on my life.
Moon (Starveling)	*This lanthorn doth the hornèd moon present.* — 155
Demetrius	He should have worn the horns on his head.
Moon (Starveling)	*This lanthorn doth the hornèd moon present.*
	Myself the man i' the moon do seem to be. —
Theseus	This is the greatest error of all the rest. The man should be put into the lanthorn. How is it else the man i' the moon? 161
Hippolyta	I am aweary of this moon. Would he would change!
Theseus	It appears, by his small light of discretion, that he is in the wane. But yet in courtesy, in all reason, we must stay the time. 165
Lysander	Proceed Moon.
Starveling	All that I have to say, is, to tell you that the lanthorn is the moon, I, the man in the moon, this thorn-bush my thorn-bush, and this dog, my dog.
	Enter Thisbe.
Thisbe (Flute)	*This is old Ninny's tomb. Where is my love?* 170
Snug (Lion)	O —
	The Lion roars. Thisbe drops her mantle and runs off.
Demetrius	Well roared, Lion.
Theseus	Well run, Thisbe.
Hippolyta	Well shone Moon. Truly, the moon shines with a good grace. 175
	Snug, as the Lion, shakes Thisbe's mantle, then exits.
Theseus	Well moused, Lion.
	Enter Bottom as Pyramus.
Pyramus (Bottom)	*Sweet Moon, I thank thee for thy sunny beams,*
	I thank thee, Moon, for shining now so bright;

152 *fell*: fierce

156 **horns on his head:** the horns of a cuckold whose wife is unfaithful

164 **in courtesy:** out of politeness
164 **in all reason:** it's only reasonable
165 **stay the time:** sit it out

176 **moused:** shaken [Thisbe's cloak], as a cat shakes a mouse

Pyramus lies dead in Thisbe's lap.
Which of Thisbe's lines do you think she was most likely to be saying when this photograph was taken?

2 How is the script for *Pyramus and Thisbe* different from the language of Theseus and the rest of the audience?

	For by thy gracious, golden, glittering beams,	
	I trust to take of truest Thisbe sight.	**180**
	But stay, O spite! But mark, poor knight,	
	What dreadful dole is here?	**182 dole:** misery
	Eyes, do you see? How can it be?	
	O dainty duck! O dear!	
	Thy mantle good, what, stained with blood?	**185**
Theseus	This passion, and the death of a dear friend, would go near to make a man look sad.	**186 passion:** fit of grief **186 friend:** could be used to mean 'lover'
Hippolyta	Beshrew my heart, but I pity the man.	**188 Beshrew:** curse
Pyramus (Bottom)	*O wherefore, Nature, didst thou lions frame?*	**189 frame:** create
	Since lion vile hath here deflowered my dear.	**190** **190 deflowered:** taken the virginity of [he means 'devoured']
	Which is — no, no — which was the fairest dame	
	That lived, that loved, that liked, that looked with cheer.	**192–3 looked with cheer:** smiled
	Come tears, confound. Out sword, and wound	
	The pap of Pyramus.	**195** **195 pap:** breast
	Ay, that left pap, where heart doth hop.	
	[Stabbing himself.] Thus die I, thus, thus, thus.	
	Now am I dead, now am I fled,	
	My soul is in the sky.	
	Tongue, lose thy light, Moon take thy flight,	**200** **200 Tongue:** [he means 'eye']
	Exit Starveling.	
	Now die, die, die, die, die. *[He dies.]*	
Theseus	With the help of a surgeon he might yet recover, and prove an ass.	**203 prove:** turn out to be
Hippolyta	How chance Moonshine is gone before Thisbe comes back and finds her lover?	**205**
	Enter Flute as Thisbe.	
Theseus	She will find him by starlight. Here she comes and her passion ends the play.	
Hippolyta	Methinks she should not use a long one for such a Pyramus. I hope she will be brief.	
Lysander	She hath spied him already with those sweet eyes.	**210**
Thisbe (Flute)	*Asleep my love? What, dead, my dove?*	
	O Pyramus arise!	
	Speak, speak. Quite dumb? Dead, dead? A tomb	
	Must cover thy sweet eyes.	
	These lily lips, this cherry nose,	**215**
	These yellow cowslip cheeks	
	Are gone, are gone. Lovers make moan.	
	His eyes were green as leeks.	
	Tongue, not a word. Come, trusty sword,	
	Come blade, my breast imbrue.	**220** **220 imbrue:** stab

'Adieu, adieu, adieu.' The play finishes as Thisbe dies. Snug and Quince are in the background. What do their expressions tell you about how they think the performance has gone?

And farewell friends, [Stabbing herself.] thus Thisbe
ends.
Adieu, adieu, adieu.

Theseus   Moonshine and Lion are left to bury the dead.

Demetrius   Ay, and Wall too.   225

Bottom   *[Starting up.]* No, I assure you, the wall is down
that parted their fathers. Will it please you to see the
Epilogue, or to hear a Bergomask dance between two
of our company?

Theseus   No Epilogue, I pray you, for your play needs no excuse.   230
Never excuse. For when the players are all dead, there
need none to be blamed. But come, your Bergomask.
Let your Epilogue alone.

Enter Quince, Snout, Snug and Starveling; they
are joined by Bottom and Flute. Two of them
dance. Then they exit.

The iron tongue of midnight hath told twelve.   234
Lovers, to bed, 'tis almost fairy time.   *Exit all.*

Enter Oberon and Titania, with all their
followers, and Puck.

Oberon   Through the house give glimmering light,
By the dead and drowsy fire,
Every elf and fairy sprite,
Hop as light as bird from briar,
And this ditty after me,   240
Sing and dance it trippingly.

[Oberon leads the fairies in a song and dance.]

All   *Now, until the break of day,*
Through this house each fairy stray.
To the best bride-bed will we,
Which by us shall blessèd be.   245
And the issue there create
Ever shall be fortunate.
So shall all the couples three
Ever true in loving be.

They all exit, except Puck.

Puck   If we shadows have offended,   250
Think but this, and all is mended,
That you have but slumbered here,
While these visions did appear.
And this weak and idle theme,
No more yielding but a dream,   255
Gentles, do not reprehend.
If you pardon, we will mend.

228 Bergomask dance: a comic
country dance
228 between: performed by

234 iron tongue: clapper of a bell
234 told: counted

240 ditty: song
241 trippingly: lightly

244 best: most important

246 issue: children
246 create: created

250 shadows: double meaning:
1) fairies; 2) actors
251 mended: put right
252 slumbered: slept
254 idle: trivial
254 theme: story
255 no more yielding but: means as
little as
256 Gentles: ladies and gentlemen
256 reprehend: tell us off
257 mend: put it right

Which of his lines do you think he was saying when this photograph was taken?

And as I am an honest Puck,
If we have unearnèd luck
Now to 'scape the serpent's tongue,   **260**
We will make amends ere long.
Else the Puck a liar call.
So good night unto you all.
Give me your hands, if we be friends,
And Robin shall restore amends.   *He exits.* **265**

260 **'scape:** escape
260 **the serpent's tongue:** hissing from the audience
261 **make amends:** make it up to you
261 **ere:** before
264 **Give me your hands:** clap your hands
265 **Robin:** Robin Goodfellow, another name for Puck
265 **restore amends:** make it up to you

These questions are about all of Act 5 Scene 1.

3 How is the comedy of the *Pyramus and Thisbe* play created through the words used by the actors?

4 How should Bottom and the others move and speak as they perform the play?

5 How does what Theseus and the others say tell you what they think of the performance?

6 In Shakespeare's time there was a great difference between wealthy and important people and ordinary people. How would this have made the audience at the time find the scene amusing?

7 How does the Pyramus and Thisbe story develop the theme of love in the play? Consider the similarities and differences between it and the other lovers.

8 What do we learn about Hippolyta's character from how she behaves and what she says in this scene?

These questions ask you to reflect on all of Act 5.

a) How do the words and images used by all the characters in Act 5 create different feelings?

b) Read lines 78–102. How would you advise the Mechanicals to behave while Peter Quince tells the story of Pyramus and Thisbe?

c) How does the final scene show a modern audience how the different social groups in the Athens of the play viewed and behaved towards one another?

d) How do Theseus' words and actions in the final scene show the audience what sort of ruler he is?

e) How does the song and Puck's final speech bring the themes of the play to a conclusion?

How to do well in assessment

Most importantly, you should aim to enjoy the Shakespeare play that you are reading, and start to think about why Shakespeare makes the characters act as they do and what the main themes of the story are. You should also begin to consider the language that Shakespeare uses. This is also a great start for studying Shakespeare at GCSE.

There are a series of skills that will help you in any assessment of your understanding of a Shakespeare play. They are:

- Read, understand and respond to the play clearly. Comment on the characters' behaviour and motivations, using evidence from the text.

In other words, you need to show that you know the play and can answer the question that you have been given.

- Analyse the language, form and structure that Shakespeare uses. Show your understanding of Shakespeare's techniques by explaining their effects. Use subject terminology.

Here, you show that you understand how the play has been written by commenting on the words and techniques that Shakespeare uses. Also, you should demonstrate that you understand and can use appropriate technical language.

- Show understanding of the relationship between the play and the context in which it was written.

You must show that you understand the connections between the text and the time that it was written. This could be historical events, like the Gunpowder Plot, but also people's social and cultural beliefs of the time – such as a belief in witches - and how these affect the way that the characters think and behave.

- Use a range of vocabulary and sentence structures for clarity, purpose and effect, with accurate spelling and punctuation.

This means that your work should be clear, organised and well-written. You are not expected to have perfect spelling, but you should spell key words and character names correctly and use correct grammar.

Advice for answering questions

Remember the skills that have explained above. You will usually not have to show every single skill in every answer that you write. For example, extract questions usually require you to cover the first two skills – commenting on characters' behaviour and looking at how the play has been written. Remember that there is not one perfect answer to any question. Consider how you feel about the characters' actions. It is perfectly acceptable to use phrases such as, 'I think,' 'I feel that' and 'In my opinion' when answering. The most thoughtful responses often show originality, but remember to support your points with sensible argument and evidence from *A Midsummer Night's Dream*.

1 Read Act 3 Scene 1 lines 70–102 (pages 43–5). How does Shakespeare create mood and atmosphere in this extract?

Considering characters' behaviour

- Make a list of the characters in this extract and list their thoughts and feelings. For example, Bottom: *confused*, *irritated*; Titania: *enchanted*, *devoted*.

- Find evidence from the text to back your ideas up.

- Explain your ideas by showing what you think each quote could reveal about the characters and what kind of mood and atmosphere this creates. Remember, it is up to you to decide what kinds of mood there are. For example:

I think that a mood of confusion is created when Bottom says, '*Why do they run away?*' because he is unaware that he has an ass's head. A mood of fear builds up when Quince exclaims, '*Bless thee, Bottom, bless thee!*' showing his panic but also concern for his friend.

Considering language and technique

To develop the skill of analysing Shakespeare's language and technique, look back at each quote you have selected and explain how these create atmosphere. Bottom thinks the workmen's scared reaction is a trick they are playing, so he asks lots of questions. His friends' shock is shown in their frequent exclamations. There are also plays on words and double meanings, as Bottom's language shows he understands less of what is going on, than the audience. For example:

Shakespeare creates comedy by using words that can be interpreted in different ways. Bottom thinks that the workmen's fear is false and is a, '*knavery of them to make me afeard*'. The irony here is that the, 'knavery' is Puck's and that the workmen are genuinely frightened. Bottom insults Snout's fearful reaction and says he only sees his own, '*ass head*'. This creates a humorous mood because Bottom is actually the ass.

2 Read Act 1 Scene 1 lines 18-51 (pages 7-9). How does Shakespeare present the theme of obedience in this extract?

Considering character

- Make three lists, one each for Egeus, Hermia and Theseus, noting how they speak and behave. For example, Egeus: *agitated*, *indignant*; Hermia: *bold*, *defiant*; Theseus: *controlling*, *insistent*. Decide which characters behave similarly or differently from each other.

- Find evidence from the text to back your ideas up. For example, Egeus is agitated in,'*Full of vexation come I*'; Hermia is bold when Theseus tells her that Demetrius is a good man and she replies, '*So is Lysander*'.

- Now build on your ideas by explaining what each example shows the audience about the theme of obedience. For example:

Shakespeare presents the theme of obedience through Egeus' anger. This is shown in the line, '*Full of vexation come I*'. Egeus is agitated because Hermia is being disobedient. He is so angry that he is taking his complaint to the Duke of Athens.

Considering language and technique

Comment on Shakespeare's technique and word choices for the characters, and their effect. The courtiers speak in iambic pentameter (ten syllables a line); but one line is split between Theseus and Hermia. Consider the effect. For example:

Theseus supports Egeus, saying Demetrius is, *'worthy'*. Hermia replies, *'So is Lysander'*, contradicting her father's wishes. This line of iambic pentameter is only completed by Theseus' answer, *'In himself he is'*, which shows his quick opposition to her disobedience.

Considering context

Consider if the characters' behaviour or language could be affected by the beliefs and expected behaviour of the time. For example:

Most fathers chose their daughter's husbands at the time, which is why Egeus is so angry when Hermia chooses Lysander. Egeus' comment, *'As she is mine, I may dispose of her'* shows what life was like for women in Shakespeare's time.

3 How does Shakespeare present the relationship between Oberon and Titania at different points in the play?

Considering a character's behaviour

- Consider what kind of a relationship it is, and its role in the play. List the ways Oberon and Titania behave towards each other. For example: *argumentative, vengeful, sympathetic.* The couple's row upsets nature; Oberon drugs Titania, then Lysander and Demetrius; Titania's love, keeps Bottom in the wood.

- List four scenes that show different aspects of the relationship, such as Oberon's jealousy and Titania's stubbornness. Find evidence from each scene to support your views. For example: Titania is stubborn in Act 2 Scene 1 when she will not give Oberon the changeling boy, insisting, *'The Fairy Land buys not the child of me'*. Does their relationship help us understand themes in the play such as love or appearance and reality?

Considering language and technique

Choose one scene from your list and think about the language Shakespeare gives Oberon and Titania to use when they speak to and about each other. For example, in Act 2 Scene 1, Oberon calls Titania, *'proud'* and, *'rash'*. By contrast, he calls her, *'my sweet queen'* in Act 4 Scene 1. What so these adjectives suggest about Oberon's attitude to Titania and why has his opinion of her changed so much?

Considering context

Consider how the relationship could be affected by beliefs of the time. Oberon punishes Titania disobedience; wifely obedience was expected in Shakespeare's time. Belief in the influence of fairies is shown by their argument muddling the seasons.

Putting your ideas together

The relationship between Oberon and Titania changes. Shakespeare shows the marriage as acrimonious when the play starts. Oberon calls Titania, *'proud'*, implying she is too arrogant to consider his feelings. He says he only wants, *'a little changeling boy'* and makes her sound unnecessarily stubborn. However, when Titania explains why she keeps the boy, Oberon seems selfish. He believes his wife should obey him; showing male attitudes at the time.

Points to remember

You should:

- answer the question, not spend ages retelling the story
- use short, focused quotes
- explain techniques, not just find them.

Practice questions

1 **Read Act 3 Scene 2, lines 166–192 (page 57). How does Shakespeare present conflict in this extract?**

Helena	Ay, do persever. Counterfeit sad looks,	
	Make mouths upon me when I turn my back,	
	Wink each at other, hold the sweet jest up.	
	If you have any pity, grace, or manners,	
	You would not make me such an argument.	**170**
	But fare ye well. 'Tis partly my own fault,	
	Which death or absence soon shall remedy.	
Lysander	Stay, gentle Helena, hear my excuse,	
	My love, my life, my soul, fair Helena!	
Helena	O excellent!	
Hermia	Sweet, do not scorn her so.	**175**
Lysander	Helen, I love thee, by my life, I do.	
	I swear by that which I will lose for thee,	
	To prove him false, that says I love thee not.	
Demetrius	I say I love thee more than he can do.	
Lysander	If thou say so, withdraw and prove it too.	**180**
Demetrius	Quick, come!	
Hermia	Lysander, whereto tends all this?	
	Hermia clings to Lysander.	
Lysander	Hang off thou cat, thou burr. Vile thing let loose,	
	Or I will shake thee from me like a serpent.	
Hermia	Why are you grown so rude? What change is this	
	Sweet love?	
Lysander	Thy love? Out, tawny Tartar, out!	**185**
	Out loathed medicine! O hated potion hence!	
Hermia	Do you not jest?	
Helena	Yes sooth, and so do you.	
Lysander	Demetrius, I will keep my word with thee.	
Demetrius	I would I had your bond, for I perceive	
	A weak bond holds you. I'll not trust your word.	**190**
Lysander	What, should I hurt her, strike her, kill her dead?	
	Although I hate her, I'll not harm her so.	

2 **How does Shakespeare present the character of Puck in *A Midsummer Night's Dream*?**

3 **Lysander says, '*The course of true love never did run smooth*'. How is the theme of love presented in *A Midsummer Night's Dream*?**

Globe Education Shorter Shakespeare

Series Editors: Paul Shuter, Georghia Ellinas

Contributors: Kevin Dyke, Jennifer Edwards, Jane Sheldon, Jane Shuter, Paul Shuter and, for the original text, Hayley Bartley, Hilary Crain, Paul Shuter, Patrick Spottiswoode.

The text of this edition is based on the text of *Globe Education Shakespeare: A Midsummer Night's Dream* (Hodder Education, 2012) and has been developed from the cut produced by Bill Buckhurst for the 2012 *Playing Shakespeare with Deutsche Bank production of A Midsummer Night's Dream.*

This book is dedicated to Bill Buckhurst and the cast, crew and creatives of the 2012 Playing Shakespeare with Deutsche Bank production of A Midsummer Night's Dream, who made this play live for thousands of London school students.

Playing Shakespeare with Deutsche Bank is Globe Education's flagship project for London schools, with 20,000 free tickets given to students for a full-scale Shakespeare production created specifically for young people. **www.playingshakespeare.org**

Photo credits

All photographs are from the Shakespeare's Globe photo library. Full details of the cast and creatives of the featured productions can be found at www.shakespearesglobe.com/ShorterTwelfthNight

Manuel Harlan, 2008 production: 14, 16, 18, 20, 22 (bottom left), 26, 28, 32, 34, 36, 38, 40, 42, 44, 46 (bottom left), 52 (both), 54, 56, 58 (both), 60 (both), 66, 72, 74, 78 (top), 82 (top), 84 (left), 90
Ellie Kurttz, 2012 production: 6, 8, 10, 12, 22 (bottom right), 24, 30, 46 (bottom right), 50, 62, 64, 68, 70 (both), 76, 78, 80 (bottom), 82 (bottom), 86, 88
Steve Tanner, 2016 production: 22 (top left), 46 (top left), 48
Pete Le May: 4

Every effort has been made to trace all copyright holders, but if any have been inadvertently overlooked the Publishers will be pleased to make the necessary arrangements at the first opportunity.

Orders: please contact Bookpoint Ltd, 130 Milton Park, Abingdon, Oxon OX14 4SB.

Telephone: (44) 01235 827720. Fax: (44) 01235 400454. Lines are open 9.00 – 5.00, Monday to Saturday, with a 24-hour message answering service.

Visit our website at www.hoddereducation.co.uk

© The Shakespeare Globe Trust, 2017

First published in 2017 by

Hodder Education,

An Hachette UK Company
Carmelite House
50 Victoria Embankment
London EC4Y 0DZ

Impression number   5   4   3

Year   2020   2019

Cover photograph (left to right) Paul Hunter as Bottom, Jonathan Bond as Snout, Sam Parks as Starveling, Peter Bankolé as Flute, 2008 production, photograph Manuel Harlan

Typeset in ITC Century Light 10pt by DC Graphic Design Limited, Hextable Village, Kent

Printed in Dubai

A catalogue record for this title is available from the British Library

ISBN: 978 1471 89375 9